To Kennique :
thank you for your
support

**Shattered: How everything came
together when it all fell apart**

Cover Art: Lisa Vallejos
Cover photo: Eden Basquez
Headshot: Sara Smith Garcia

Shattered: How everything came together when it all fell apart

ISBN: 9781796756845
Imprint: Independently published

Acknowledgments

This book wouldn't be possible without the support and unwavering support of a few key players who have guided me, shaped me and helped mold me.

Dr. Tom Greening whose term "existential shattering" gave a name to what I'd experienced. With his support and blessing, I was able to run with this idea of shattering and to carry the torch forward.

Dr. Louis Hoffman who has and does still believe in me sometimes more than I've believed in myself. Louis is a mentor, colleague and it is my honor to call him my friend. Dr. Shawn Rubin, whose unwavering love, support, encouragement & humor have kept me grounded while he encourages me to soar. Dr. Donna Rockwell, who has become like a mother to me and whose leadership I will always follow. Dr. Dave St. John, my friend and colleague. Dr. Sandy Sela-Smith, who created the method with which I studied my dissertation research, whose editing helped my dissertation become what it was and whose kindness held a light in the darkness.

My friends: Laurie, Veronica, Susan, Trish, Monica, Derrick, Vanessa, Rich, Candice, Laura, Nisreen...all of you held me down at some point and in some way. Thank you.

My family: for racing to the hospital, to sitting with us for long days & for being an anchor. I love you.

Dedication

To Gabriel & Eden:

You two are the best part of life. You always have, and
continue, to make me braver than I knew was possible
& stronger than I dared believe.

To Denay:

For everything, for always.

This book is dedicated to the memory of Kylie Grace. You are my hero.

The beginning

I knew I was pregnant before I even missed a period. My body started showing me signs within a week of conception and I took a test to confirm my suspicions before I was even late. When those two pink lines crossed the stick, I felt a mixture of excitement and horror. The father of the baby growing in my belly was someone I barely knew; he was the son of a woman I'd worked with and befriended and our fling was the cliché "good girls like bad boys" scenario. He was handsome, dangerous and the exact wrong guy for me and now, I was pregnant.

Not having this baby never even crossed my mind; I knew from the minute I suspected I was pregnant that this baby would be born, with or without the support of its father. I was more than capable of taking care of a child on my own—I had a Master's degree in Counseling, a career and was close to being a Licensed Professional Counselor and knew that even if it wouldn't be easy, I could do it.

The baby's father was surprised to discover I was pregnant and seemed fine to defer to me and even though we didn't have much of a relationship together, we began the journey of becoming parents. We lived separately and both had jobs that consumed a lot of our time. To say our beginning, as a family was unconventional would be an understatement. We were two virtual strangers who were now becoming parents.

I never wanted to have kids or get married. It just wasn't something I'd considered up to that point because I was focused on other things; I was married to my education and career and I had dreams for what my professional life would look like. There was no room for a family in the life I had planned for myself. I had a dog, family and friends, and for me, that was more than enough.

The decision was made and I would be come a mom. It was odd to prepare for this new adventure and what made it even more odd was that although I was pregnant and knew I was pregnant, nothing had really changed. I had a tiny belly, nothing more than I had after overindulging at Chipotle and was still wearing my normal clothes. My breasts were sore but nothing more than PMS symptoms. I had only experienced minor morning sickness and it was rare. If it weren't for the ultrasound photos showing me the proof of the life inside of me, I might not have believed it myself.

On a beautiful September day in Denver, Colorado, I was scheduled for my first full ultrasound. I was 21 weeks by this time and barely had a belly to show. I pulled on my usual jeans, a long sleeve tee and headed out the door.

Fall in Colorado is gorgeous as the trees begin changing colors and the mountaintops in the distance turn white with snow. I was up early because I was anxious. Today would be the day that I would see the baby I was carrying for the first time in detail. I wondered what would be revealed in the photos—if the baby would look like his father or like me. I desperately wanted to know the gender of the baby but was debating keeping it a surprise until the baby was born.

It was the early afternoon as the baby's father and I made our way to the hospital ultrasound clinic. We laughed, joked and bantered on the way, nervous excitement filling the car. We arrived, I checked in and we were promptly escorted back to the ultrasound room. The technician was a woman with a lingering Russian accent who quickly became part of our celebration as she pointed out different features of the baby. She'd say "here's the hand—the baby is waving saying 'hi mom'". It was absolutely beautiful to see the little being growing inside of me.

After about 15 minutes of looking, the tech grew very quiet. She intensely peered at the screen and the humor left her face. Feelings of trepidation began to rise within me and I tried to push them back down. Shortly after, she told me that she was finished for now but asked me not to leave, saying she might need to take more pictures. I returned to the waiting room, nervous and unsure but trying to pretend that everything was ok. I was floating down the river of Denial and I was a long way from Egypt. The lightness I'd felt only moments before was beginning to be replaced with an unnamed dread.

Shortly after, I was called back in. When I entered the room, there was a man sitting next to the ultrasound machine wearing a white coat that was embroidered with "head of ultrasound". He asked me to lie on the bed and he began to look at the baby. I felt as though I'd swallowed a gallon of ice water and I knew without doubt that something was dreadfully wrong. Tears began streaming down my face in the silent, dark room. Perhaps he was moved by compassion because he stopped, looked at me and said the words that would forever alter my life. He said "I'm not a doctor so I can't give you a diagnosis but I can tell you there appears to be something wrong with your baby's heart". Grief like I've never felt before filled my entire body and I began to cry from a place I didn't know existed inside of me. I remember walking out to the parking lot, and although it was not a cold day, my memory of it is that it was overcast and heavy. I recall watching cars that were driving by, people laughing, DJs joking on their radios, and wanting to scream at the world, *"How dare you go on without me!* I felt like a bomb had just exploded in my life, and the dust had not yet settled. The dust of my emotional world exploding settled down around me as the person I used to be crumbled into someone I'd yet to meet.

I can't recall what exactly was said after that but I left knowing that he was sending the images to the midwife practice where I was receiving my prenatal care for review. Although I was 21 weeks along at this point, I'd not seen a physician as I opted to have my care as natural and noninvasive as possible. I don't think I'd ever actually seen a physician in the office before and only knew they were a part of the practice by their names on the door. On the way home, I tried to convince myself that it was going to be ok, that maybe it was a mistake and maybe there was nothing to it. Deep inside, I knew I was wrong.

Later that day, I got a call from a number I instantly recognized as the midwife practice. I answered with a dry mouth and the voice on the other end introduced himself as "Doctor" and again, the seriousness of what we was happening sunk in a little deeper. It was a real doctor calling, not a nurse or a midwife. This was a big deal. He couldn't or wouldn't tell me exactly what was wrong but stated that he was making a referral to a specialty obstetrics group and that I would need to get into see them as quickly as possible. Numbly, I agreed.

Although I couldn't tell you exactly what the ultrasound technician and head of ultrasound looked like, or their names or anything else, my mind narrowed in on their conversation enough to pick up a few words that I logged in my mental notebook. Despite the big feelings of that day, I kept my wits enough to listen carefully to what was being whispered. Armed with only "hypo-something" and "heart problems in babies" I went to my computer, opened the screen and began to type.

Thus began my foray into the world of Congenital Heart Defects. With the tiny bit of information I had, I was able to find some information and what I found terrified me. I'd entered an alternate, parallel universe where babies were born sick and sometimes died. I wanted desperately out and into my old world. Like Alice in Wonderland, I had fallen into a hole and didn't much care for or understand my new surroundings.

I quickly learned that there was a name for babies born with heart issues and that it was "congenital heart defects" (CHD). I also learned that about 1 in 100 babies in the USA are born with a CHD and that some of them never live to see their first birthday. Although there are well over 100 different types of CHD, the little big of information I had gleaned in the ultrasound room told me a chilling story about the likely future of my unborn baby.

There are only two CHD's with the prefix "hypo" in them—hypoplastic left heart syndrome (HLHS) and hypoplastic right heart syndrome (HRHS) and both are extremely serious conditions. The treatment for both includes at least one invasive heart surgery designed to redirect the blood flow, lifelong medications and ongoing visits to a cardiologist. Although the outcomes are better now than they were 20 years ago, they are still not great. And to be honest—any chance of my baby not surviving was too much for me to consider. Everything within me rebelled at this information and I desperately wanted it to be something else.

After spending hours scouring the internet, looking for something other than what I already knew, I did the only thing I could think of: I called my mom. She answered and immediately, a flood of emotion and tears overtook me and I began to cry. She said "Lisa, what's wrong" and I was finally able to choke out the words "there's something wrong with the babies heart".

She said, "I'm on my way".

Right before the diagnosis, I had started my first semester as a doctoral student, studying psychology. I loved the challenging work and the feeling of gaining new knowledge. School suited me well and I was thriving. Two days after the ultrasound, I drove to the school I was attending and sat in class. I was numb and unable to focus. At the break, I spoke to my instructor and despite my best efforts at remaining composed, I burst into tears as I shared that I was facing the hardest thing I could have imagined. Suddenly, school seemed empty and pointless as I was now fighting for my child's life.

When I left class that evening, it was the last time I would set foot on that campus as a student. I left school and my dream behind to focus on doing whatever was necessary to take care of this child. I suppose even then I knew that come hell or high water, I was in this thing for good.

My mother arrived from Houston the following evening, less than 24 hours after my desperate call. Between me crying and speculating about the baby, we shifted into gear. Suddenly, things I'd not even considered were weighing heavily on me. Before, I had always considered medical insurance an afterthought and was never terribly concerned about my coverage. Now, I was frantic with worry because I needed medical insurance to guarantee the health of my child. I'd always been a person who made my own choices and decided my own fate and suddenly, I was at the mercy of this unknown diagnosis and the insurance personnel who would make decisions about his care and mine without knowing us. I called my insurance company to ask about coverage and encountered a distant woman who seemed to be reading out of a manual. The longer I spoke with her, the more upset I became until I finally shoved the phone into my mother's hand and asked her to finish the call for me. Sobbing, I ran into the bathroom and promptly vomited. I was terrified.

Only a few days passed between the ultrasound and the appointment I had with the neonatologist but I felt like I'd aged a lifetime. I went to the appointment, anxious. During the appointment, the physician and his staff were nice and did a full workup on my baby. I still didn't know the gender of the baby. When they asked me if they could perform an amniocentesis and explained the risks, I was hesitant but they wanted to be sure of what was going on with the baby as often CHD shows up with other birth defects. Reluctantly, I agreed. The fear I felt when the doctor approached me with a foot long needle was mild compared to the fear I felt wondering what he would tell me about my baby.

After the exam, the doctor told me that my baby had what appeared to be a Hypoplastic Left Heart, which is where the left side of the heart never grows. My baby's heart had a severely under formed left ventricle and atrium. Without those two things, the baby's heart could not get oxygenated blood to the rest of the body. The doctor offered this as a preliminary diagnosis and promptly made an urgent referral to a pediatric cardiologist, an appointment that was to take place within days. I was unsure about why there was such a sense of urgency but I complied with what was asked.

On the day of the appointment, I waited in the cardiologist's office with my family, including my parents, brother, sister in law and niece and nephew and various members of my partner's family. We laughed, joked and made conversation, studiously avoiding anything significant or challenging. When I was called back to the exam room, I entered with mounting levels of anxiety. The pediatric cardiologist was a large, well-dressed Black man who was clearly very good at his job. His demeanor was professional and he was impeccable in his appearance. He examined my baby's heart thoroughly and when he was finished, he turned to me and confirmed my fears. My baby did indeed have HLHS. The cardiologist then went on to inform me of my options, which I fondly refer to shitty options 1-4. The first option was to have an abortion but if I decided to go that route, I only had a short time to decide as my pregnancy was advanced. It suddenly made sense why everything was so urgent.

The second option was to do what's known as palliative care, which is when the baby is born and offered no medical intervention. In that case, the baby would die naturally within about 10 days. The third option was to have a series of corrective heart surgeries known as the Norwood and Fontan. The last option was to have the baby and try to get a heart transplant.

I kept asking questions, hoping the doctor could give me better guidance. Truthfully, I really wanted him to tell me exactly what to do that would save my baby. I wanted an answer from someone who knew better than me what the outcome could be. Of course, there was no way he could do that but in my desperation, I wanted a quick and easy answer. Most of my life had come with some sort of manual—the Bible as a guide for living, the counseling ethics code to help me make tough clinical choices and syllabi to show me exactly what I was expected to do. Here, in this most dark place, there was no manual, no reference point and no one to tell me what to do. The choice was mine alone and there was no way to tell me where my choice might lead. As a child who looked ahead in Choose Your Own Adventure books to know how to choose my best path, this was nothing I'd ever experienced and I felt out of my depth.

Leaving the doctors office and walking to the lobby where my family waited was one of the longest walks of my life. The hardest part was sitting here with this stoic man who was telling me that I might want to consider abortion because I was "young enough to start over". I felt like he had probably seen this a million times before and was jaded to the process. He knew the odds were against the baby surviving and was perhaps trying to spare me the pain of that. But even though he might have seen this before, it was my first time. It was MY life. It was MY baby.

My mind was cluttered and the easy answer I wanted from the cardiologist never came. The diagnosis was not a mistake, this situation was real and I had to accept it. When I saw my family waiting in the lobby, the looks on their faces made it all too real. The weight of grief finally hit me in full force and my knees gave out beneath me. I quite literally fell into the lap of my parents, sobs wrenching from my body, my young niece rubbing my back while my brother sat quietly with tears in his eyes. I remained there for a long time. I wasn't ready to stand. I wasn't ready to face this.

I wasn't sure I would ever be okay again.

Free Falling

I was now in an all out free-fall into the strange land of congenital heart defects. The weeks following the diagnosis were filled with appointments, blood draws, ultrasounds, meetings and being inundated with information. In the time I wasn't getting poked and prodded, I was scouring the Internet, trying to find answers, which was both a gift and a curse. I knew enough to not be surprised my much but what I was learning was terrifying. The more I knew, the bleaker the outcome seemed.

What I found was nothing less than terrifying. I discovered that there are many different types of CHDs. They range from mild to severe with the most severe requiring at least one invasive heart surgery during the patient's life. As many as 1 in 100 children, or 1% of live births, are diagnosed with a CHD, and 48% of those children diagnosed with CHD die in infancy[1] and

---

[1] Gilboa, S., Salemi, J., Nembhard, W., Fixler, D., & Correa, A. (2010). Mortality resulting from congenital heart disease among children and adults in the United States, 1996 to 2006. *Circulation, 122,* 2254–2263.

70% of those deaths occur within the first 28 days of life[2]. There doesn't seem to be a genetic link and when I asked the cardiologist what caused my babies heart defect, he looked me in the eye and said "bad luck". Honestly, I would have felt better if I had a reason for the diagnosis because it would have given me an enemy. It would have given me a target for my feelings of anger. Bad luck meant there was no reason...there was no enemy and somehow, I'd drawn the short straw. Intellectually, I knew that life "isn't fair" but that didn't provide any comfort. I wasn't special, I wasn't protected, I wasn't exempt from sorrow and my notion that being a good person meant I'd experience good things was clearly wrong.

I fell deeper into the rabbit hole of congenital heart defects as I researched my options. The first two options, to do nothing and to let the baby die naturally or to get an abortion seemed unthinkable. How could I possibly give up without even giving this baby a fighting chance? I was already deeply in love with this baby and couldn't imagine giving up so easily. This

---

[2] Centers for Disease Control and Prevention (CDC). (2014). *Congenital heart defects* (CHDs). Retrieved from www.cdc.gov

baby, not even fully formed and already so sick, had completely captured my heart and soul. The thought of a lifetime without him or her was not something I could imagine. I refused to roll over and accept this. I refused to live forever knowing I'd given up and always wondered what might have been. I decided I'd rather give him or her a shot and know that I'd done everything I could have done. I'd rather live forever with the broken heart of losing a child than to never even give him or her a chance.

The next option was to undergo a series of corrective heart surgeries where the surgeon would redirect the blood flow of the heart. The baby would have the first surgery shortly after birth, the next a few months later and the next at about three years old. As I considered this option, I imagined my tiny baby having its chest cut open so many times and the thought made me ill. I began looking into heart transplant surgery.

A few weeks after the appointment at the neonatologist's office, I received a call regarding the results of the amniocentesis. The doctor informed me that other than the heart issue, the baby was perfectly normal. The baby had no chromosomal issues and seemed to be perfectly healthy. When I got this news, I was relieved. I asked the doctor what the baby's gender was and he asked me "are you sure you want to know?"

I said yes and after a moment's hesitation, he said, "it's a boy". I laughed and cried as I realized that I was carrying a son.

During this time, I was heavily involved in a Christian church where I had a lot of friends who served as a great support system. I believed in the power of prayer and relied on my faith to help me cope. I truly believed that God was going to heal my son and I held fast to that belief, no matter how bad the situation looked on the surface. One night, I stayed up all night praying, quite literally begging God to either save by baby or take him now. I prayed and cried and prayed and cried and finally fell into an exhausted, restless sleep. When I didn't have a miscarriage the next day, I took it to mean that God was going to save the baby. I was expecting a miracle.

A few weeks after the diagnosis came, I went to a movie called "Facing the Giants". This movie was produced by a Christian church and was a faith-based tale of a coupe that was facing challenging circumstances. The movie tells their story but there is one scene in particular that struck me. In this scene, the protagonist, a high school
football coach challenges his best player to do a death crawl, which is crawling on hands and feet with another player holding onto his back. The trick is that the coach

blindfolds him. As this scene unfolds, the player begins and crawls five yards, then ten, then further. His body weakens and his resolve starts to fade and when he is nearing the end of his strength, he begins to cry out how he can't go any further. The coach drops to his knees beside him and begins yelling at the player "don't give up! Don't give up! Don't you dare give up on me! It's all heart from here!" The player digs deeper, conquers his limits and collapses in the end zone, completely exhausted. When he removes his blindfold and sees how far he got, he and his teammates are in awe.

I wept through that entire scene because I felt like he did—I was exhausted, scared and already felt defeated by my own life circumstances. There was a part of me that just wanted to give up but I took the message from that movie and as I cried in that dark theater, I realized that in my life, the only thing that would get me through was the sheer will to survive.

I walked out knowing that for me too, it was all heart from here.

The next few months were uneventful. The baby's father and I moved into the same apartment to ease the financial burden that would come with his birth. We were in a strange position because we had never really decided to be a couple; we just slid into it because our life circumstances required it. We were simply doing what needed to be done for our child.

Although the appointments continued, they were less frequent as the doctors knew what was going on and all that needed to happen was for me to decide what course of action to take. It wasn't an easy process for me as I researched every possible article I could find, seeking answers. I didn't know it at the time but being well informed was, for me, a form of defense. I felt that the more I knew, the more control I might have over the outcome—after all, knowledge is power and in my most powerless state, I desperately craved a sense of power over *anything*.

After weeks of agonizing over what to do, I made a decision. I decided to go for the heart transplant option because it seemed the best chance for him to live with the minimal amount of surgeries. The thought of sending my baby into heart surgery so many times was more than I could bear. I've never been much of a gambler but in this case, I was all in. I was going for broke and although I knew the chances of him getting a heart were small, it seemed the best option with the least amount of pain.

That decision made, I began searching out the best transplant programs in the US. My search directed me to Children's Hospital of Philadelphia, which was listed as the top Pediatric Heart Transplant program in the nation. I called and left a message for a transplant coordinator, inquiring about their program and wondering what I would have to do to get my son treated there. A few days later, she called me back and we spoke shortly about the diagnosis and situation. She asked where I lived and when I said Denver, she said "Are you aware that Denver Children's Hospital has one of the best transplant programs in the country"? I wasn't and was quite surprised to hear that. She said, "Let me call my contact there and pass on your information".

It was just a few days later that I got a call from the Heart Institute representative, who would soon become our families Transplant Coordinator. Within a couple of weeks, I was sitting at a conference table filled with medical professionals and a social worker that were explaining the whole transplant process to me. I was doing my best to remain detached and clinical in the discussion. Many times, I felt as though I was discussing someone else's life, not mine. I spoke with the physicians, nurses and social worker and was bantering, making jokes and overall, likely didn't have the demeanor one would expect from a mother whose child's life was at risk.

I was super skilled at hiding how I felt and it was serving me well.

I grew up in a large family. I was born to a single mother and an alcoholic father, with my mother on welfare and living in what we referred to as "The Projects"—our community version of public housing. My grandmother, the matriarch, had birthed 10 children and raised 9 (one died early in infancy). Because my father was either absent or raging, the responsibility of raising my brother and me became a family affair. We spent most of our days with our Grandmother, Aunts and cousins while my mother worked. It was a sparse life but I didn't know it. I only knew that the summertime afternoons when my mother would slice up watermelons and we would sit on the porch, the juice running down our arms to the ant piles below were some of the best.

My family was built on strong women who became strong because they needed to be. To hear my mother and her siblings describe childhood was both funny and tragic. They lived in a small house, and many times, their relations with each other were more of a war zone than a safe place. My grandmother, rest her soul, did the best she could do with the resources she had. Sometimes, that included throwing cutlery and using electric cords to get kids in line.

That sort of upbringing, no matter the love that is present, comes with a price. The price is that one must be tough because to be weak will make you a target. That toughness is one thing I remember most of my own childhood...I rarely saw any of the women in my family cry. The only time I can really remember any of them crying was when major tragedy would strike and that was infrequent.

I was a sensitive child and was easily hurt by the sarcasm, digs and snide comments that would pepper the conversation in my childhood. When it finally became to be too much, I made a vow. I swore I would become harder so that I wouldn't be hurt so easily. I promised myself not to be so damn sensitive and learned how to lob the digs with the best of them. I learned how to "ignore" the sarcasm that would still poison my spirit. I learned how to absorb the pain and pretend it didn't hurt.

By the time I was sitting in children's hospital, hearing the potential outcomes for my son's life, I was an expert at masking my feelings. I was so out of touch with how I felt that it was almost as though I was dissociated.

After that meeting with the transplant team, there was nothing to do but wait. I was only about 26 weeks at this point and had another 14 weeks to go before the baby would be born. It was hard to live my life as though it were normal because I knew that what was coming was anything BUT normal. Yet, I still woke up every day and went to work. I still went for walks in the park with my dog. I tried to go about my life as routinely as possible and all the while, felt odd because what my family was facing was nuclear. It wasn't normal. It wasn't ok. Yet, there was nothing on the outside yet to suggest otherwise so I kept living my life.

I went to a Neonatologist every other week for ultrasounds and checkups for the baby. Each time I went, I hoped for a miracle, that the doctor would do an ultrasound and discover that it was all a mistake or that somehow, his heart had grown whole. Of course, it never happened but I never stopped wishing for it.

During this time, my sister in law Traci started to plan for a baby shower. As I was the recipient, I was not involved in the process. One day, I got a call from my Traci, frustrated because she was getting nowhere in the planning because none of my aunts or cousins would call her back. At a loss, she enlisted my help.

I called my Aunt and asked her what was going on and why no one was helping Traci plan. She said, "we didn't want to have a baby shower because we are worried about how it would impact you if you were to have all that baby stuff around as a reminder if the baby doesn't make it". I immediately burst into tears and said "it's not your decision to make...don't you realize that if the baby doesn't make it, every breath I take for the rest of my life will be a reminder"?

After I stopped crying, I called Traci back to tell her to go ahead and plan the shower and to forget family participation. Although I didn't know it yet, this was the first crack in the foundation of my family relationship that would soon crumble.

The rest of the pregnancy proceeded without incident. The baby slowly grew and my life seemed to stabilize a bit. I continued to go to work and live my life as normally as possible. I began to plan for him by prepping a nursery, buying necessary items and thinking about a name that would suit him. I tossed around naming him after his father but that didn't seem right. It was always in the back of my mind—what name would suit this little boy that was entering this world already so wounded? It had to be perfect because to me, a name is a declaration. Each time you speak someone's name, you are affirming a truth about who they are and this name had to be a bold statement. It had to fit him and his destiny just right.

It was about this time that I began to notice that I was having trouble focusing. My mind was constantly pulled back to the war that was waging inside of my emotions. I would vacillate between terror and faith. I had trouble sleeping, eating and would often feel depressed and hopeless. One morning at work, it struck me that I was experiencing nearly all of the classic symptoms of Post Traumatic Stress Disorder. I went to a colleague's office, another therapist, and mentioned my thoughts to him. I said, "Brian, I am experiencing all of the symptoms of PTSD" and he looked over his wire-rimmed gasses and said, sardonically, "ya think"? I laughed and yet realized that I needed support. There was no way my faith, professional knowledge and church would get me through this. I asked some colleagues and got a referral for a therapist. I called him immediately and set an appointment for later that week.

I began seeing Bill regularly and while some of the work we did was about the pregnancy and the upcoming birth, much more of it was around my relationship with the baby's father. We were not suited to be a couple and in fact, had been apart before the baby's diagnosis. It was only then that we began trying to have a traditional relationship and were forced to move into the same space to consolidate costs. We both knew that the baby's medical condition would require around the clock care that would mostly fall to me.

I spoke often to Bill about my feelings of powerlessness and helplessness. He was a kind man; a good therapist and he held my trauma carefully. I was a fragile, brittle woman sitting in his office, wound tightly and held together by willpower and grit. I would often say to Bill that falling apart was a luxury I didn't have. I simply wouldn't allow myself to go there—I thought that if I did, I might never come back together.

The baby's due date was February 7, 2007. In December, I began going into the neonatologist weekly. The baby was not growing as much as the doctor would have liked and so I had a talk with the baby about growing a little bigger. "Hey buddy, this is your mommy here. The doctor would like to see you a bit bigger when you're born and you're not growing fast enough. You think you can do something about that, sweetheart? I know, crazy, right?

By this time, I'd chosen his name, which would be Gabriel Gideon. Gabriel is his father's middle name and Gideon came to me as I was driving and listening to a Christian CD. A song that I'd heard many times before came on and as the first refrain of the lyrics were sung, I got goose bumps all over my body. The lyrics said, "The Lord is with you Mighty Warrior, so arise". When I arrived home, I went immediately to the Bible and turned to the book of Judges where the tale of Gideon is told. The verse states "then an angel of the Lord appeared to Gideon and said "the Lord is with you, Mighty Warrior" and goes onto tell how Gideon, following the Lord's instructions, led a small army of 300 to defeat an army 10 times its size. As I read the story, I thought of the baby growing in my womb and the odds against him. What better name to give him than one whose legacy is about a Warrior who beats the odds?

This was it. This was his name. He would be called Gabriel Gideon; meaning God is my strength and Mighty Warrior. At least with his name, he was well armed. The rest remained unknown.

About a week after the little talk I'd had with Gabriel about his growth, I went in for another ultrasound. He'd gained almost a full pound after my little pep talk, which explained my increasing levels of discomfort. He was now 6 pounds and I was still a month away from my due date. The next week, he'd also gained a pound and was now a little over seven pounds. When I went in the third week after our talk, our Neonatologist looked at me after measuring Gabriel's head and said, "I'm concerned that now that he's growing so much that you may not be able to deliver him. His head is as big as his stomach. If he gets much bigger, you may have to have a C-section and I know we'd both prefer to avoid that".

The plans to induce labor began. We got preregistered at the hospital that day, the neonatal intensive care unit was notified and we called our families. I had already prepared my delivery bag and in less than 48 hours, Gabriel's father drove me to the hospital where I would spend the night alone, to be induced at 6 a.m.

❖

I didn't sleep much that night. I was restless, worried and tried to assuage my fears by reading and praying. I finally fell asleep only to be awakened by a nurse what seemed to be only a few minutes later. She injected the Pitocin into my IV and the process began. As the hours went by, family members arrived and came to say hello. The contractions increased in intensity but my water hadn't yet broken so at about 9 am, the neonatologist came in and broke it for me to speed up the process. They wanted Gabriel to be born before the shift change happened in the afternoon and since my previous talk with him and gone so well, I whispered to my baby boy "Gabriel, if you can come before noon that would be great". The room, filled with family members, medical professionals and a news crew waited anxiously.

The last part of labor was hard and I wasn't sure I could do it. I'd decided some point before delivery that I wasn't going to get medicated. I wanted to be fully alert when he was born—I wanted to remember every detail of his arrival. As I thought about his delivery in the weeks before, I thought about the women who had gone before me, my ancestors. I thought of the women who went out into the woods, squatted and delivered babies on their own and cut the umbilical cord with their teeth. I thought of how strong a woman must be to do that, and I realized that I am descended from a bloodline of fierce women. Tapping into that space within me, drawing on the ancestors before me, I decided to have a natural birth. I believed, on a core level, that if I could do the most painful thing a woman experiences without medication, then in the process of delivery, there would be a divine osmosis that would happen. The strength in me would go into Gabriel, empowering him to fight his own battle.

Gabriel Gideon entered this world at 11:17 a.m., a large baby for 38 weeks at 8 pounds, 8 ounces. He was beautifully pink with the chubbiest cheeks I'd seen. Immediately after he was born, the medical team jumped into action while my delivery doctor tried to stop my bleeding. Although I didn't know it at the time, I was hemorrhaging and the physician was concerned but was able to stop the bleeding relatively quickly. I knew something was wrong by the look on my mothers face and how quickly she turned away from me while the doctor tended to me.

The doctor brought Gabriel to me and I held him for what felt like just a few seconds, as the medical staff stood by, waiting anxiously to take him to the

NICU. Although it broke my heart to let him go, I handed him to his father who, in tears, carried him down the hall to the NICU while our family and friends lined the halls outside of my room, hoping to catch a glimpse of Gabriel as he passed. Nobody knew when, or if, they would ever see him again.

I was cold, and tired so my nurse gave my hot chocolate, some soup and covered me with blankets. I fell asleep for about an hour and then when I woke, demanded to be taken to the NICU. Of course, the medical staff preferred that I continue resting but there was no way in hell I was going to not be with my child.

When I got into the NICU, Gabriel was in a Plexiglas crib with cords attached to both feet, an IV in his hand and a blood pressure cuff on his ankle. He was so tiny in there and I felt an ache all the way to my bones, wishing I could shield him from the path ahead. Only grandparents, aunts, uncles and parents were allowed in the NICU and visitors were only allowed a couple at a time, so there was a rotation of people who came in and out during the next few hours. I sat, holding my son as often as I was able between medical professionals coming in to evaluate him.

I stayed with him as long as I could but eventually had to go back to my room to sleep. I came back to the NICU the next morning, ready to get him prepared for discharge to Children's Hospital. After Gabriel was born, my mother was given the task of contacting Gabriel's Transplant Coordinator at Children's Hospital to let them know he was born. When the doctor confirmed that I was ready to be discharged, we had to wait for a bed to open at Children's Hospital. It was a long day of waiting but the call finally came; a bed was ready and it was time to transfer Gabriel to Children's Hospital.

About an hour later, a flurry of activity catches my eye outside of the NICU and I see a group of people in Flight for Life gear pushing a bright orange crib. The sight of them made my stomach clench up and my heart jumped to my throat. The seriousness of what we were facing hit me like a ton of bricks. They came into the NICU and I remember the parents in the NICU looking at me and then averting their eyes. It was almost as if they had a sense of relief that it wasn't their child being taken by Flight for Life but then felt guilty about feeling relief.

This was the first time I felt disembodied, as if I was watching myself from the outside. I watched them prepare to move my son as I stood back quietly. When he was ready, they wheeled him out of the NICU and down the hall. Alone, I followed them and I watched as people pressed themselves against the walls as we passed. In their eyes, I saw a mixture of pity and gratitude. At one point, I remember thinking, "how is this my life"?

On the ride to Children's Hospital, I sat in the back with Gabriel. It was only a few blocks away so the ride didn't take long. When we arrived at Children's Hospital, the intake process began quickly. Within a short while, Gabriel was admitted, I was given a matching parent wristband and we were escorted upstairs to the NICU. There, the intake nurse arrived and began assessing Gabriel. Again, he was such a trooper and hardly fussed as she examined him. He got his first blood transfusion that night, as the medical team wanted to test how his body handled foreign bodies. This would give them an indication of how his body would handle the transplant we were hoping for.

I prepared to stay in the reclining chair in his little room, which was really just a small space cordoned off with curtains when the nurse strongly encouraged me to go home. She said "I know you don't want to leave and I totally understand it but there's nothing you can do for him here. He will sleep, I'll be with him and he really needs you to be well rested and taken care of as this is a marathon, not a sprint". After some cajoling from her and Gabriel's father, I finally agreed to go home to sleep. Walking out to the car, I was choked up the entire time and by the time I sat in the passenger seat, the tears were flowing down my face. I felt I was abandoning my child and I felt like the worst mother in the world.

The next few days went by in a blur. I would wake up early in the morning, take a quick shower, and rush Gabriel's father to get to the hospital. I would spend the days sitting in the reclining chair, holding Gabriel and learning all about his medical needs. My mother camped out in the lobby and would rotate with me when necessary. I'd go out to eat or take a quick nap, and she would go sit with Gabriel. He was never without family during the days. We had friends come and deliver food or just to visit. The cardiology team would come on rounds daily and assess Gabriel's progress. He was given different medications, and was eventually put onto Carbon Dioxide to lower his oxygen levels. In a baby with Gabriel's heart condition, the main focus in the first few days is keeping the ductus arteriosus open. The ductus arteriosus is the blood vessel between the pulmonary artery and aorta and is how blood gets to the rest of the body. With the combination of prostaglandins and reduced levels of oxygen, the ductus arteriousis remains open and allows blood flow to continue.

During rounds, it was much of the same information daily but about a week after he was born, Gabriel started to decline. He hadn't been able to burse at all from the time he was born because he just wasn't strong enough. He would latch on and stay latched on but lacked the strength to nurse. I tried everything I could do to get him to nurse and it never worked. I pumped regularly and we would feed him out of a small bottle. He could only take a few ounces at a time and that amount began to diminish.

Gab slowly began looking more and more sick. His fingernails began to turn blue, a sign of his lowered oxygen levels. His body was chilled and it would take longer to get him warm again. When he would cry, he would struggle to breathe and his cries were weaker. Gabriel would lie listless in my arms. As his body began to fail him, my anxiety rose. Now, the cardiac team looked more worried and we began to discuss whether he would be a good candidate to have a shunt put into his heart to facilitate continued blood flow through his heart to his body. My prayers increased and I would quietly beg God for a miracle. I wondered if he would get a heart transplant in time to save his life.

When I would think about Gabriel getting a heart transplant, I would feel equal parts hope and grief. I felt as though my prayers to save his life were also a prayer for another mom, somewhere, to lose her child. I grappled with these thoughts because while I realized that it was a necessary path to Gabriel's wholeness, I wondered if I would be to blame when it finally happened.

❖

On the thirteenth day after he was born, I was holding Gabriel in my arms, doing Kangaroo Care, which is holding a baby skin to skin. His body was cold again and I knew my own body heat would warm him again. I snuggled him up to me and covered him up with a pile of blankets. I slowly rocked the chair and he fell asleep. As he rested peacefully, I began to relax and soon began to doze off.

I was startled awake when the curtain to his room was pulled aside. It was the duty nurse and she said to me, "you have a phone call". Groggy and confused, I looked for my cell phone and began to stand up. My mind cleared and I looked closer at her eyes. They were glossy with tears.

My heart began to pound in my chest. I shakily handed Gabriel to her and made my way to the nurse's station. When I arrived, another nurse handed me the phone, took the call off of hold and I said a shaky "hello?" The voice on the other end was one I recognized. It was one of the transplant coordinators that I had spoken to many times during rounds. She said, "I'm calling to let you know that we got a call and there's a heart available for Gabriel. We are flying out soon to check on its viability and we will know for sure in a few hours if it's a good match. If it is, we will be flying back to Denver tonight and performing the surgery. In the meantime, we are going to get Gabriel prepared for surgery and we will let you know as soon as we know". I don't recall what I said but the call ended and I slowly walked back to Gabriel's room.

I was shocked and stunned because while I always believed it would happen, I never expected it to happen this soon. When I got back, I grabbed my cell phone, and the nurse handed Gabriel back to me. I called Gabriel's father, my mother, and my brother and let them know it was happening. My brother left work immediately and began the drive to the hospital. He had been sick when Gabriel was born and hadn't yet seen him so he wanted to be there to see him before the surgery.

The remainder of the day was a rush of activity, as staff came in and evaluated Gabriel, taking blood draws and making sure everything was in place. After what seemed like the millionth poke, Gabriel's veins collapsed and the staff attempted to place an I.V. in his head. I couldn't bear it anymore and told them to stop. He needed a break. He needed to be held by his Mama and truthfully, Mama just needed to hold him. Everyone left the room and it was just Gabriel and I. I rocked him, sang to him, read to him and poured all the love I had within onto him and then even more. I prayed for him and I wept again for the family who was saying goodbye to their baby.

A few hours later, the surgeon came into meet me and tell me what the plan would be. I had to sign consent forms, and state that I understood the risks. The doctor told me how the surgery would go. He told me that he would get Gabriel ready for surgery before the heart arrived so that when it did, they could do the surgery immediately. He explained what would happen afterward and while I understood what he was saying, I was a bit numb from everything.

When the surgeon came in the room, I was taken aback at how young he looked. He was wearing the standard issue blue scrubs and had a mast hanging around his neck. I noticed he was wearing black crocs and for some reason, it seemed funny to me. Although he seemed young, he quickly took command of the room and began explaining how surgery would go. There was a local news team present who had followed our story and the producer really wanted to be in the surgery room to film. She asked, he said no and she asked again. He looked at her sharply and said, "We do not want anything in the room that can disrupt the flow of the surgery. You will not be allowed in". His rebuke was swift and sharp and the force with which he delivered it was reassuring to me. I knew then that this was a man who was not playing around. He was serious, diligent and careful. My confidence in him increased and I was oddly comforted. As I began to sign the forms, he looked at me, gentler and in his eyes, I saw both compassion and confidence. He said "I promise you I will not leave this hospital until I am 100% confident that everything is as it should be and that your son is doing well". He didn't even mention the other possibility.

My brother and sister in law were close when the surgery was about to begin. They were pulling into the parking lot when the anesthesiologist came into explain the procedure to me. I asked them to stall for a moment so my brother could arrive. They stood back a bit and agreed to wait. A nurses aid offered to go to the parking garage and get them. She ran out of the room, down the hall to the elevators to find them and they rushed back to the room. My brother came rushing in, and was able to hold Gabriel for a few moments and he told him how much he loved him. When it was time to go, Gabriel was placed back in his crib, the wheels were unlocked and we began the trek to the operating theatre. As we walked, Gabriel was strangely calm which calmed me. He stared at me, never breaking eye contact and I stared into his eyes. As they opened the operating room door, I kissed him, told him how much I loved him and that I would see him soon. I didn't cry, even though I knew it might be the last time I saw him alive.

We went into the waiting room and people began playing cards and other games. We were studiously trying to keep our minds occupied. I had one of Gabriel's blankets and I lay on the floor. Oddly, I was able to fall asleep. When the hourly update came, the transplant coordinator informed us that Gabriel was sedated and getting prepped for surgery.

As we were in the waiting room, outside of the hospital another drama was unfolding. The heart transplant team charters a private airplane from a small airfield in South Denver Metro. When the heart team is arriving with a heart to transplant, they call ahead to the tower and are given priority landing. This may mean having other flights circle the area until the heart plane lands. When they land, the team disembarks with a cooler, just like you'd take to a picnic but in it, lays the heart. They get out of the plane and rush to the ambulance that is waiting. They get in, get secured and take off quickly to the hospital. A police car will often clear the path before the ambulance as they race the clock. A heart is only viable for four hours after being harvested from the donor, which means that any delays can render an organ unusable. When the heart team arrives to the hospital, they burst through the emergency room and race off to the operating room.

Heart surgery is serious business. The process begins with anesthesia and then, my son's body was cooled down to slow the blood flow. He was placed in an ice bath and the surgeon began the process of cutting through his breastbone. When the breastbone is cut, the chest is opened wide. There, he remained until the new heart was close enough to begin removing his old one. During this time, Gabriel was on a bypass machine which functions as a heart, taking in oxygen poor blood and returning oxygen rich blood. Once his heart was connected to the bypass machine, he was given a medicine to stop his heartbeat. During this surgery, Gabriel was also given blood thinners to prevent blood clotting. The surgeon then used a tube to remove the remaining blood from his heart and the bypass machine took over by pumping the blood back into his body. The surgeon carefully began excising the broken heart, cutting the veins and arteries carefully to ensure he'd be able to reattach them to the new one.

The updates came every hour: *his chest is open, his old heart is out, the surgeon is placing his new heart now, the surgeon is connecting his arteries, the surgeon is almost done, the chest is being closed now, his heart is in and beating but not as well as we'd like, which is normal, so he's placing an external pacemaker to keep it going, his chest is closed and he will be going to the Cardiac Intensive Care Unit (CICU) for recovery soon. We'll come get you when you can see him.*

Between those updates, I would either rest beneath Gabriel's blanket or busy myself talking with others. Throughout the night, various family members and friends came and went. A friend from high school arrived in the early morning hours, bearing food and drinks. I was calm and collected, even able to joke and make light of the situation. I saw other families waiting around and wondered about their situation. To my surprise, a handful of the staff that was off duty stayed around through the night to remain updated on Gabriel's progress. I suddenly remembered my dog, Dori, was at home and became worried. She needed to eat and go for a walk but no one wanted to leave the hospital to take care of her. Thankfully, one of the nurses who were waiting with us volunteered to go walk her on her way home. Gratefully, I handed over my keys and gave her instructions. I was blown away by the generosity and support we received.

My parents were there and my dad had a cold. I told him to go rest in the parent room that was reserved for me and as I walked with him, he burst into wracking sobs. The hours of tension and fear were for him in his physically weakened state, too much to bear. He was terrified, for Gabriel and for me and oddly enough, I reassured him as I walked with him to the room. I told him we would come get him when we knew more but told him not to worry...I was sure Gabriel was just fine. I knew in the very depths of my soul that if something had gone wrong, I would be able to feel it.

The TV crew wanted an interview so we sat down and they set up. It was the early morning hours and as the camera rolled, I shared what was happening. I was composed and calm until she asked me the question "if you could say something to the donor family, what would you say"? I burst into tears and said "I would say, thank you and that I promise I will make sure he lives a life that makes the sacrifice meaningful". That was the only time that night that I cried.

At a little before 4 a.m., the nurse came to get us and Gabriel's father and I were escorted back to the Cardiac ICU. We washed our hands, showed our bands and the nurse's assistant took us back to him. She pulled the curtain back and nothing could have prepared me for what I saw. Gabriel was lying on the crib, with a ventilator in place and so many cords connected to his body that I couldn't begin to count them. There were two I.V. poles beside his bed and they were stacked with medications flooding his body. He was naked and he was so swollen that he looked three times his normal size. His eyes were taped shut and he was heavily sedated. The most jarring thing was that his chest was still partly open with nothing but a piece of white Tyvex sewn in to hide his heart but I could still see his new heart beating in his chest beneath it. The Tyvex rose and fell, rose and fell and its movement mesmerized me.

The only thing I could touch on his body was his toe and so I did. I spoke to him, told him how brave he was being and how proud I was of him. I told him that I would be with him through it all. When I spoke to him, his heart rate rose slightly and the nurse said, "he knows you're here". It gave me great comfort to hear that and when she encouraged me to leave so that he could rest peacefully and without raising his blood pressure, I complied. I didn't want to do anything that would risk his recovery.

When we left the CICU, as we stepped into the hall, Gabriel's father burst into tears and nearly fell to his knees as the enormity of what he saw with our son hit him. Sobbing, he said "I can't, I can't" and I reassured him that he didn't have to; I was there and I wouldn't leave Gabriel's side. The moment passed and he gathered himself. We walked down the hall and I decided then that I didn't want anyone else to see Gabriel in this state because it was truly horrifying. I didn't want anyone else to have to hold that memory of him in that state in his or her mind.

As we left the CICU, we passed the surgeon. It took me a moment to recognize him in street clothes but when we made eye contact, I knew it was he. He was wearing jeans, and a leather jacket and what jumped out to me were his boat shoes. Although neither of us said a word, seeing him in his street clothes and hearing his words from just a few hours earlier echoing in my mind told me that all was well with Gabriel. I knew this man wouldn't leave if there were even a small chance that something was wrong. Seeing him step into the elevator gave me a deep sense of peace and reassurance.

I went to a parent's room down the hall and slept fitfully for a few hours. I woke up and immediately went back to the CICU. Because I knew he would know I was there, I only said hi to him and then sat quietly next to his bed. I didn't want to excite him by talking to him or touching him, so I sat, trying to read and barely absorbing the words on the pages. I sat in that same chair for the next 72 hours, leaving only to quickly eat, grab a drink, and use the bathroom and sleep. After three days, the nurse encouraged me to get out of the hospital for a short while so I went across the street to get a coffee. It was the first time I'd been outside in days, or even out of the same hall, and the sun seemed extra bright.

I finally went home that night to sleep, as the hospital had limited parent rooms available and other families needed them for their child's surgery. The next morning, I was awakened by a call from the hospital and a physician on the other end let me know that they had taken Gabriel early in the morning and closed his chest fully, as the swelling had reduced enough for them to know the heart fit well. He told me when I arrived; Gabriel would have staples in his chest instead of the Tyvex.

I rushed to get ready and to get to him. Within an hour, I was there, by his side and looking at his tiny chest, closed with 15 giant staples. My heart broke for him, and the pain he was in. I once again wished I could take it all for him. The medical staff was beginning to lower the narcotics he was receiving to wean him completely. He was off the ventilator and was breathing on his own, with oxygen. The pacemaker was still in place and he'd yet to awaken yet. Still, I sat with him day and night because there was no way I would miss him waking. I wanted to be the first person he saw when he woke up.

He finally woke a couple of days later and as I hoped, I was by his bedside. He looked at me and I looked at him. My miracle baby was back in the land of the living, now carrying someone else's heart in his chest. I couldn't be more grateful. Now, our task was to wean him off of the narcotics, manage his pain and help his body take over its natural functions again.

Within a week, Gabriel was moved to the step down care unit where I learned how to care for him now. He got sponge baths and we had to be careful to avoid the tape holding his chest together. He was on a nasogastric (NG) feeding tube, which is a tube that goes into the nose, down the throat and into the stomach, as he wasn't able to eat. I had to learn how to prime a feeding pump, dose his post-transplant medications, what to watch for, how to hold him because the surgery made his chest so painful that traditional holds were painful. We waited for his first post-surgery bowel movement because that is one of the signs that his body is functioning normally again. When he finally pooped, we all cheered. Every little victory was celebrated, as he inched a little further from death daily.

When the medical team finally felt he was ready to go home, there was one final hurdle to jump. I had to learn how to place the NG tube in case it fell out at home. A nurse came into the room, took out his tube and walked me through placing the tube. It was awful. Gabriel screamed and fought me every step of the way. When I was finally done, and checked to make sure it was done properly, I was shaking and horrified. I promised him I would never do that to him again and held him to me as I soothed both of us.

On the tenth day after his surgery, we went home. He wore a little red sweater and blue sweat pants. We packed our stuff, loaded the car and then placed Gabriel in his car set. We walked out, carrying our little Warrior to the car. I was ecstatic and terrified. I wondered if I had what it takes to care for him. I wasn't sure I was ready but I knew I needed to be.

Gabriel continued to improve and I was happy with his progress. Shortly after coming home, his NG tube that fed him was pulled out by accident one early Friday morning before clinic, and his transplant coordinator decided that we could leave it out over the weekend. Between Friday and Monday, now eating from a bottle, he gained almost a pound. Delighted, we kept feeding him strictly by bottle and he began to grow. Gabriel's weight had stabilized and his growth chart flat lined shortly after he was born and now, the line on his chart was climbing steadily up. We were thrilled to see him grow.

One morning, Gabriel's dad looked at me and said, "We should get married". I was surprised but agreed. I'd never really considered getting married before but given that we were living together and had a child together, it seemed like the right thing to do. We went ring shopping that afternoon and planned a backyard wedding for three days later.

We got married in his dad's backyard, by a fountain. It was March so still chilly outside but this Sunday was nicer than usual. Our parents were there and it was a happy day, with food, dancing and music. It seemed like we were on the right track and that life was on the upswing. I was now a married woman and a mother, both things I had never expected to be. We seemed like a dream come true.

It wasn't going to last. A week after we got married, the ghosts from his past began to haunt us. Within two months, I felt betrayed and trapped in a marriage that I didn't want to be in but I couldn't see my way out. Some things came to light that had I known, I may not have made the choice to get married. I felt betrayed and resentful because I felt that had he been honest with me up front, I could have made the decisions knowing what I was getting into it. As it stood, his lies and deception robbed me of my freedom to choose freely. I hated him for taking my choice from me. I hated him for trapping me in a situation that I felt I couldn't leave; after all, the time had passed for an annulment and divorce wasn't an option. I tried to move beyond it to save our marriage and our family. It was one of the hardest things I'd faced.

I went back to work part time as a therapist, re-enrolled in my doctorate training and things seemed to settle. My marriage was still not going well—we barely kept afloat and it soon became necessary to have extra support. My husband's income was inconsistent and not enough so we often struggled. I was extremely resentful at being forced to go back to work and having to hire a nanny to take care of Gabriel. I wanted to be with him and take care of him but there was no way we would make it if I didn't work. Eventually, I asked my mother to come back to Colorado to help us out because I didn't know how I would sustain without her help.

We had friends, a church family and soon moved into a bigger home. Things seemed to be going well on the surface but there were constant issues going on just under the surface. We seemed to be a power couple, the ideal family, and the paragon of what a married couple should be but there was constant turmoil. The truth is that we were not happy as a couple and we were both trying to force it. We got married on a whim because it seemed to be the right thing to do and now, we both knew it wasn't the best decision. We were trying to be something neither of us was, trying to live up to the expectations of those around us. On some level, we loved each other but it was more about loving the idea of the other. We didn't KNOW each other to know if we loved the other. We loved our hopes. We loved our dreams. We loved our fantasy.

We adjusted to our life and routine. The routine consisted of going to the hospital for clinic three times a week, administering a plethora of medication around the clock and trying to be as normal as possible. I was still pumping breast milk every few hours to feed Gabriel and would often try to nurse, but he wasn't able to do it. It was a heartbreaking thing for me as I had always dreamed of nursing my baby. When I couldn't, I felt like a failure.

That changed one day when we were out. Gabriel got hungry and his bottle just wouldn't warm. I was sitting in the backseat with him as he cried and I decided I would try to nurse him. I took him out of his seat, lifted my shirt and lifted him to my breast. TO my shock and amazement, he immediately latched on and began nursing like he had been his whole life. I wept with joy. It was these moments that kept me going when everything seemed so bleak.

Unknown to the people around me, during this time I was grappling with a deep sense of despair. It wasn't something I could freely name because as a "woman of faith", I wasn't supposed to feel hopeless and despairing.

My child was alive. What else could I want?

It wasn't that simple. While I was grateful for his life, I was wrestling with feelings I could hardly face, much less name. I was grateful for his life, and at the same time, terrified that death would come knocking any moment. I was grateful for his donor, and felt wracked with guilt. My child was alive because another woman's child wasn't. My marriage was a sham, and my family abandoned me when I needed them most. My faith was crumbling. The very foundation upon which I'd built my life was coming apart, brick by brick and I couldn't keep it together.

One day, the wall I'd built to hold it all back broke and all the feelings I'd held in came bursting out. While Gabriel slept in my arms, I stared at his face and began reflecting on what we had been through and what still was to come. Although we were married, I was miserable and knew that I had made the wrong choice in getting married. I was socially isolated because I was terrified to take Gabriel out in public because of his immune system being compromised, and my family support had begun to crack. I loved Gabriel with a depth I never knew was possible, and I knew he was the best thing that had ever happened in my life. As I pondered the depth of my love for him, I realized that the very depth of my love could be the thing that would destroy me if I lost him.

How can one climb to the very heights of love and survive devastation when the object of that love is gone? I was sure I would never survive losing him. As I imagined what my life would be like if he died, the thought filled me with panic and grief. I could barely manage to breathe. Tears streamed down my face, and

I silently sobbed while my heart felt shredded inside of me. The most terrifying thought came to me—that perhaps it would be better for me to strap him in his car seat and drive off the edge of a steep mountain. Then we could die together, and I would never have to feel the pain of losing him.

This was not the first time in my life that I wondered whether death would be a better alternative to living; however, this time I was not only thinking of ending my own life but my son's. I was embarrassed and terrified that my thoughts went this way. As I entertained these thoughts, I reached for the book that had always provided me with clarity; *Existential Psychotherapy*[3], and I began reading. When I read, "Though the physicality of death destroys us, the idea of death saves us", I knew I had a big decision to make. I went for a drive later that evening, alone, and thought seriously about death. I actually played out the fantasy in my head of driving Gabriel and me up to a high mountain, holding him in my arms, and driving as fast as I could off the edge. I wondered what would happen if one of us happened to survive. I wondered how my

---

[3] Yalom, I. (1980). *Existential psychotherapy*. New York, NY: Basic Books.

family and friends would feel. I imagined the devastation that my parents would feel. I wondered about my brother and his children and how such a thing would impact them.

That evening, I chose to live. I reached toward life with a hesitant hand hoping life would reach back. The next morning, I called Gabriel's transplant coordinator and asked her what his limitations were and what I could do with him. I found out I could take him swimming and delighted, I went to the store to get him swim trunks, diaper, a hat and a baby float. I looked at his beautiful eyes and I made a commitment to him that day: I promised him that whether he lived to be 8 or 80, I would make sure that his life would be one hell of a journey.

When I chose to live, it wasn't enough just to be alive...we needed to thrive. We had to make the pain worthwhile. What kind of life would it be for him, or for me, to live trapped in a little apartment because I was afraid of going out in public and getting him sick. What kind of life was it to be if I let fear control my life and his? What would happen if I spent however much of a life he had, trying to keep him a safe little bubble?

No. I refused to spend his life, and the sacrifice of his donor being ruled by fear. In my decision to live, I defiantly raised a fist at Death. Sure, Death would come for both of us eventually. But it wouldn't find us cowering in a corner somewhere, hoping to hide from it. When Death came for us, it would have to search the mountaintops, the rivers and the valleys. It would have to seek us out by listening for the music of laughter that comes from overflowing hearts. It would not find us fearful but would find us triumphant, knowing that with every chance we had, we lived. The choice to live fully was easy; the path to getting there was not.

In October, the next big blows came. My maternal grandfather fell ill and died after a week in the hospital. The day he died, I received a call from an Aunt who was upset with me for inadvertently sharing a family secret with an unknowing cousin. Only a few days later, my maternal grandmother had a stroke and was also hospitalized. She was in the hospital for a number of days and I began to prepare for the worst.

The call came that we needed to get to the hospital immediately and I called on a friend to go pick up my mother and Gabriel and take them to the hospital, as I was at a meeting. I met them there and went into the room with my grandmother, where she was lying peacefully. A pastor from my church came into the room and began to read my Grandmother's favorite bible verse, Psalm 23. Before he finished, she took her last breath.

The next few days solidified the demise of my relationship with my family. Like many families, my grandmother was the glue that held ours together. Without her, true feelings came out and the ugliness that comes from years of keeping secrets came bursting out. My mother, brother and I were the targets. It was ugly and given that we were all still recovering from Gabriel's surgery only a few months earlier, it was even harder to be abandoned when we were all still so raw.

I'd always imagined my family as being my support system but now I realized that the support came at a cost; I would be loved and accepted as long as I didn't tell the truth about things. I would be loved and supported as long as I played by their rules. I would be loved and supported if I denied my own experiences and kept the toxic family secrets under wrap.

My brother and I spoke at length and agreed that neither one of us would agree to play their game anymore. A few weeks later, we celebrated our first Thanksgiving as our newly reconstituted family unit; he and I, our spouses, parents and children. It was the best Thanksgiving I could have imagined.

❖

I was still grappling with the guilt that still haunted me. I desperately wanted to reach out to Gabriel's donor family but every time I would sit down to write a letter, I would freeze. What could I possibly say to convey the depth of my gratitude to another mother who had buried her child, so that mine could live? Gabriel's very life was tied to the death of another and I couldn't seem to find the words I wanted to share with her. Although I knew logically that I wasn't responsible for her child's death, I couldn't untangle the knot within me that believed that somehow, I had made it happen. I wondered if my prayers for my son's life were the cause of her child's death.

I only knew that his donor was a four-month-old girl from Oklahoma. Beyond that, I was clueless. When I would allow myself to think of her, I would feel the heaviness descend within and would freeze. Each time his heart transplant anniversary would come around, I'd find myself torn between gratitude and guilt. How dare I celebrate his life when it had come at such a high price?

Finally, one night, the dam broke within me and I sat down to write the letter. I wrote about Gabriel and his health. I told her how he was doing and all the things he liked. I shared how grateful I felt but left out the guilt as I didn't feel that my guilt was her burden to bear. I sent it off, along with a photo, to the Donor Alliance who would facilitate any communication. I wasn't sure I'd hear back from her and wasn't sure I'd be able to bear her response. I wondered if she would be grateful I reached out or if she would be resentful.

I received a letter back from her in July. I got a call from the Donor Alliance who let me know they had gotten a reply. They quickly scanned the letter and the photo she sent, and I sat at my computer, breathless with excitement and fear. When it came through, I went first to the attachment of the photo and saw a beautiful baby girl with blue eyes and a small smile looking back at me. Tears filled my eyes and began slowly rolling down my cheeks. I learned she had died after a car accident, and her mother's words were so kind and loving. She shared her gratitude that Gabriel was well and expressed her desire to meet someday. I learned her name and her family composition. I learned that Gabriel's heart mom, as I called her, did not hold resentment for his life but rather, was grateful that her loss wasn't in vain. Learning that gave me a sense of relief; the guild I'd carried came rolling off my shoulders and I felt gratitude wash over me.

I didn't respond. I couldn't bring myself to reach back when I was so consumed with everything else we were facing.

The seed to fully live that was planted years before was starting to grow but I didn't know yet what my decision to live would require of me in the years to come. What I hadn't yet realized was that the foundation I'd build my life upon was insufficient to support the decision I'd made. I hadn't yet realized that my choice to live life fully was one that would challenge my life in every way possible. It had already begun, and as the bricks fell away, layer after layer was exposed.

As marriages built on fantasies tend to do, ours began to fall apart but we kept trying to keep it together. I found out in May that I was pregnant with our second child, due in December. I knew in my gut that it was a girl and I was thrilled and scared to death. Our marriage was barely holding it together now. How would another child change that and how could we possibly stay afloat with another baby when we were already drowning with one?

Being pregnant gave me something to focus on. I loved her from the moment I knew she was in my womb and I was thrilled to have another baby on the way. I didn't realize how afraid I was for her health until the day I went for a prenatal echocardiogram, standard for siblings of children born with CHD. When the echo tech placed the wand over her heart, I could see four fully formed chambers, working just as they are meant to work. I called my dad from the sidewalk outside the doctor's office and burst into tears of relief when he answered. I said 'Hi Dad. The baby's heart is just fine and I was right...it's a girl". He laughed and wept tears of joy, and gratitude with me.

By the time she was born, I knew the marriage was all but over. During her delivery, as I was in pain, her father slept in a chair. The duties of caring for me before and after delivery went mostly to my mother. After two days of labor, she burst into the room with a head full of hair and a loud cry. I held her in my arms, my perfect baby, and was flooded with joy. We named her Eden.

The next two weeks were bliss as I nursed my new daughter with ease, slept with her on my chest and napped as often as I could. My healing process with her was much quicker than with Gabriel and it opened my eyes to how much harder it was when I had him. It was like having a really amazing wine after only having boxed wine; you don't know what you were missing until you experience the other side. Everything I struggled to have with Gabriel came easy to Eden. She was the image of perfection and her birth was a catalyst to deeper healing for me. I had everything I'd wanted for Gabriel; she nursed easily, slept well and was a calm, happy baby. The things I'd grieved for with Gabriel were pieced back together with Eden. Having a normal birth with a healthy baby was a gift and I was so grateful for the experience.

Over the course of the next few months, my marriage fell apart. The children's father lost his job again and we were once again financially struggling. I tried everything I knew to do, including starting a private practice to make more money. I felt resentment every time I had to leave my babies again and by now, the anger was so deep with both of us that we could hardly stand to be around the other. Our fights grew increasingly ugly and started to turn violent. One day, after a particularly nasty argument, I jumped in my car to leave, crying and enraged and caught my own eye in the rearview mirror. I didn't recognize the woman I had become. I called his father and told him to come get him out of my house; otherwise things would be really bad. We were on the edge of doing irreparable harm to one another and it needed to stop.

Our marriage crumbled completely shortly around our second anniversary and he was out of the house for good by July. I'd tried everything; cajoling, threatening and begging but nothing seemed to get through. I finally read the writing on the wall and realized that it was over. The night he left, I laid in my bed, both children sleeping beside me and felt the hot tears streaming down my cheeks.

What the hell was I going to do?

I didn't file for divorce until September. I think there was still a part of me hoping that we could work things out. I'd grown up with a single mother and an absent father and didn't want that for my kids. I wanted to give them a happy home, with both parents loving them and being there for them. I wanted something better than what I'd had.

I finally decided to file when Eden had a procedure to have a birthmark removed from her head. She was scheduled for outpatient surgery that would remove her birthmark and be stitched up. The whole procedure should only take a few hours and would be minimal, but for a ten-month old baby, it was a significant event.

That morning, I waited for my husband to come to the house so he could drive with us to Eden's appointment. I'd told him we needed to leave by 6 a.m. and when 5:50 rolled around, I suspected he wasn't coming. When 6:00 arrived, I got in the car with Eden and left to the clinic. When he didn't arrive at the clinic or even call to see how she was doing, I knew it was over. As she rested peacefully at home after her procedure was done, I took the divorce paperwork I'd already prepared to the courthouse and filed it.

It was odd; I was clinging to a marriage that had been pretty bad the whole time. I was trying to save this marriage desperately; I asked him to go to counseling and prayed relentlessly but when I really got honest with myself, I wondered why I was trying so hard. Truthfully, I didn't even really like him as a person so it made no sense, logically. I called my therapist, the one who helped me through Gabriel's diagnosis and started counseling again.

I peeled back my skin and let everything out in those sessions. There was no censoring, filtering or hiding. I was as raw and as real as I could be. Bill quickly pointed out to me how hard I was being on myself and suggested I be more self-loving. Bill had kind eyes. I remember seeing tears and pain in his eyes as I told him some of my pain and the compassion I saw reflected there was an unspoken way of granting me the permission I needed to be compassionate to myself. Suddenly, I realized that if a client were sitting in my office were sharing my story, I'd be so much more gentle but with myself, I was constantly driving myself harder and further, demanding I do more, be more and show up more. I was truly my own worst enemy.

As I worked in therapy, I realized that I was clinging to hope, not to the actual marriage. I was invested more in my dreams than I was in the reality that was before me. It wasn't the marriage I wanted to save; it was the idea of the marriage. I'd been holding onto the fantasy that we would mend our broken fences and become the couple I'd hoped we'd become. When I finally released the fantasy and accept the reality, I was able to let go. It wasn't an easy process; embracing my new status as a divorced mom of two young children challenged my already depleted resources. I was beyond exhausted but it wasn't a tired that can be healed with rest. It was a bone-weary level of tired that I'd never felt before. I was at the end of my rope and doing my level best just to hang on.

❖

It was around this time that my spiritual foundation crumbled. I sought support through my church home during the divorce process and found the support lacking. Perhaps the circumstances of the divorce were too messy. Truthfully, I'd had questions about the Christian religion for a long time—I didn't like the dogma anymore. I'd seen so much hypocrisy within churches, church leadership and Christians that I wondered what the value of the religion was for me anymore. I no longer felt uplifted and encouraged in church; I felt defeated and down and I thought, "If this is God, I want nothing to do with him".

Slowly, I stopped going to church. I felt guilty in the beginning because it was such a huge part of my life before this. I would sleep in a little later on Sunday's and not feel rushed to get out of the house. I began to enjoy my lazy mornings on the weekends. Like many religious escapees, I rejected God because I had tied together the religion and the deity; the two were intertwined in my mind and I couldn't untangle them.

When I left the church, I also left behind many of my friends because I couldn't stomach the Christian talk anymore. I hated when people would say, "I'll pray for you" and would neglect the physical and emotional needs of others. I hated being told to "pray about it" and to "cast my cares on God". I hated the idea that in order to be "blessed", I had to be perfect.

I'd been exposed to the Christian religion my whole life, when my grandmother would read her Bible for hours on end and would sing hymns as she cleaned. We would watch Christian television and sometimes go to church together. Christianity was woven into the very fabric of my life and leaving it behind felt a bit like betrayal.

Of course, people didn't understand. Many of the people I'd known along the way struggled with my new position. Many of the friends I'd had up to this point were people I'd met while working in ministry and when I started saying things like "I don't believe that anymore", they would look at me, aghast and horrified. Many times, they would offer to pray for me, and would express concern about my soul, which I found amusing. I tried to avoid talking about religion and spirituality but I found that as I stepped more into my own truth, more of those people disappeared.

By the end of 2010, I was divorced, without my family support, without a spiritual foundation, completing a doctorate program and caring for two children on my own. I was drowning under the weight of trying to keep it all together. My entire life had crumbled and I stood in the middle, with two lives completely dependent upon me. Falling apart was a luxury I didn't have.

It was about this time that I realized I had a choice to make; I could continue on my same path, feeling down and out or I could choose a new path. Determined to change my circumstances, I realized that if I needed to start within and I decided that I was going to choose happiness, even though life was challenging. I grabbed my post it notes and wrote, "Today, I choose happiness". I gave myself until Thanksgiving to feel bad about everything that happened prior to that point and actually said to myself, "you have until Thanksgiving to feel bad, wallow in self-pity and feel sorry for yourself, so you better make it good. After that, the pity party is over and life begins again".

When my Pity Party deadline hit, I committed to choosing happiness every day. Even though it wasn't always easy, and in fact, was often very hard, I would say to myself "I choose to be happy" and would make an intentional choice to feel happy. I began to feel lighter quickly and soon, my bad days stopped lingering for weeks on end and would become just bad days. Soon, a bad moment stopped stretching into a whole day. Soon, I didn't have to choose happiness consciously anymore—I simply was happy. Well, happier.

A New Dawn
New years eve, 2011

I got the kiddos into bed and went to my room. I lit a candle, and pulled out the list I'd made earlier that day. It was a list of people I needed to forgive. On the top of the list was a familiar name; mine. I sat quietly and meditated before I opened my eyes and began to walk through a forgiveness and release ceremony. I'd held onto so much pain from the past couple of years and I knew I needed to let it go.

Rage and anger had served me well up to this point. It was the anger and need to prove myself that drove my getting a Master's Degree. It was anger that kept me from crumbling when my marriage came undone. It was anger that stiffened my spine when I had to face the challenges that came with divorce. Anger was my fuel. Anger was my friend...always there, and never let me down. Letting go of the anger and moving into forgiveness meant that I'd have to learn new ways of being strong. It meant I had to learn how to stand up for myself without shoving back so hard. It meant that I had to acknowledge the pain that I experienced, and caused, and that I had to let go of the desire for retribution. I was terrified. I wondered if I would melt into a puddle of nothingness when I released the anger and pain. I saw myself like the Wicked Witch of the East when she melted into nothingness. Who was I without pain to define me?

It turns out that forgiveness isn't a one-time event. It wasn't as simple as saying a forgiveness mantra and then magically seeing my life transform. When I began the process, I would actually say the forgiveness mantra many times a day, sometimes as many as 100. Every time something would happen that would cause pain or anger to rise, I would remind myself to breathe and say the forgiveness mantra. Perhaps if I'd been in a bubble, it would have been easier but it wasn't that simple. I still had to see my ex-husband many times weekly for his visits with the children and he still behaved in difficult ways. I had to say the forgiveness mantra many, many times when I saw him because inevitably, something would happen that would irk me. It was literally a daily practice.

It wasn't just him that I needed to forgive. There was my own family who had wounded my mother, brother and I so deeply. There were people in the church I used to attend who abandoned me when I needed them the most. There were friends who disappeared when my life became too messy. There were the people who lied to me and hid the truth from me.

       The hardest person to forgive in this time was myself. I blamed myself for much of what went wrong in my life. I blamed myself for Gabriel's heart; I thought maybe I was being punished for something I had done wrong. I blamed myself for choosing a partner who was not suitable for me. For anything that went wrong in my life, I blamed myself. I was my own harshest critic, with exacting standards that no person could ever meet. There was no room for human error for me in my mind. I had to be damn near perfect or else, I was a total failure. I said the forgiveness mantra to myself many times, and each time, I struggled with receiving it.

       About the same time, I began to tentatively reach out toward spirituality again. I'd tried the path of Atheism but it didn't work for me. There is simply too much magic in the world for me to believe it was all happenstance. I didn't know how to pray unless I was begging for something or apologizing for something else so I began to talk to the Divine (I still couldn't bring myself to call it God) in a different way.

       "Hey there, Spirit or Source or...whatever. I'm still not even sure you're real so this is kind of awkward for me. I mean, I WANT to believe you're real and I want to believe that you actually care about me but I'm a little reluctant to go there in my mind and heart. I know that asking for a sign is supposed to be sort of blasphemous but I'd really like a sign...you know, if you're really real".

An answer was not to come, at least not in the way I was expecting. I knew I wouldn't find the God I was seeking in the aisles of a church and so I began looking for alternate paths. I attended Buddhist festivals and went to get a psychic reading. I sought out alternate readings on spirituality. I began looking for God in the ordinary, and stopped expecting messages to come from a church or a pastor. No longer bound by religion, I found God in the strangest place—within.

I began to trust my intuition when it told me something was off and learned to find magic in the ordinary. I saw the divine reflected in the bird who perched on the tree outside my window, singing just after a spring snowstorm. I saw the divine in the walks I took with my children to school, as they laughed and splashed in puddles. The Divine was present in the stranger who was kind and in the seemingly effortless ways our needs were met.

No longer did I feel an unbridgeable gap between the Divine and myself and I began to explore the notion that God was within everything, even the challenges. I wondered if the divine was at work, even in the hard times, as the challenges broke me down and made me into something new. I finally took my hands off of God's throat and began to accept that maybe, Divinity was also found in the darkness. I was finally, step by step and day by day, coming out of my own dark night of the soul.

I stopped asking for a sign, and started looking at the synchronicities that showed up. In this process, I realized that I wasn't being punished for being bad, but that the challenges served a greater purpose. It forced me to my knees and stripped me of all my beliefs that didn't serve me anymore. It became apparent that the life path ahead of me wasn't one that was based on whether I was good enough, or deserving enough, or if I simply prayed enough with enough faith. My life circumstances weren't ever about my goodness; that I was good was never the question. It was whether I believed in my own goodness and would allow myself the freedom to be fully human and still, one with the divine.

One restless night, my email notification on my phone dinged and I reached for it. I opened it to find an email from someone I was not expecting to hear from; Gabriel's donor mom. Even though we were supposed to communicate via facilitated conversations through Donor Alliance, she too was curious about us and was able to locate me through the non-profit organization I'd started to support families like ours. I read her email and she stated how much she wanted to meet Gabriel. I quickly replied and our conversations became frequent. In only a few weeks, we'd made plans for her family to come to Colorado to meet ours.

Our first meeting happened at Gabriel's favorite place to visit, the Denver Aquarium. We waited outside and when they approached, I knew immediately who they were. Not sure how to approach, I introduced myself and was instantly choked up. We hugged, somewhat awkwardly and then entered the Aquarium together. Gabriel, normally a shy child, reached for her hand without hesitation and I hung back, watching my son who was carrying her daughter's heart, march off to show his heart family his favorite place.

Peace descended within and as it left, so did the guilt I'd harbored for so long. Feeling much freer from the past and the pain that had held me back for so long, I began to explore what it was that I truly wanted, not what was expected of me. I began to entertain the idea of leaving Colorado and making a fresh start and opened my heart to the idea of possibly finding love again.

❖

I began to explore the notion of having a life that was fulfilling and vibrant instead of a life where I was moving from one battle to the next. Truthfully, I was tired of feeling like I had to fight to make progress. I was tired of feeling like I was constantly in a struggle. I didn't want to be the master chess player in my life, where I was attempting to make the right move to get the right outcome; I wanted to surrender to the flow and to allow magic to happen for me. Survival mode had gotten me this far and I was ready to let it go and truly move from survival to thriving. Maya Angelou spoke to me in her words "surviving is important. Thriving is elegant". It was finally time to thrive.

I took a class called Personal Mythology at this time and it was revolutionary. The course took me deep within my psyche and into my soul, leading my to find the agreements I'd made, the personal commandments I'd been living by and oaths I'd made to myself and others, unconsciously. One of the things I learned how to do was to access my Inner Shaman (wise person) and how to step into myself, fully. I wrote this in a paper for the class:

Walking through the clearing, I become aware that the river is flowing uphill and I marvel at that awareness. I pass the Graveyard of Lost Illusions and I see headstones that say "Family" and "Innocence". I am walking toward where I will meet my Inner Shaman. The trees are lush and the ground soft. I am barefoot and can feel the coolness of the ground on my skin. I walk through the clearing and I see my Inner Shaman. She looks like a Greek Goddess; beautiful, regal and radiant. She is pleased to see me and greets me with a gentle smile. I feel somewhat unworthy standing in her presence but quickly feel my perceived dirtiness pass away. I ask her "what do I need to know to move on in my life" and she says "it was never about you". I am not sure I understand that thought but I trust that the answers will emerge with time. I ask her how I will return to her and she instructs me to simply ask for her wisdom.

As I stepped back into myself, I felt an instant change in my energy. My shoulders straightened and my posture became straight. I felt what could only be described as regality comes into me. My arms shot up, triumphant and powerful and I felt a sense of strength and softness emanating from within. I reflected that I get my satisfaction from my children and loved ones but also from my work, my studies and by expanding my world. I don't draw from only one well but from many wells that are each quite deep. My position in the world has evolved; when I was in my 20's there was a song that was popular called "Girl from the Gutter". The lyrics talk about a girl who was bullied, looked down on and rejected but who has finally become successful. The chorus line says, "I hope your hell is filled with magazines and on every page you see a big picture of me. Under every picture, the caption should read, not bad for a girl from the gutter like me". That song came into my mind as I was reflecting on my position in society as I really do see myself as a kid who was never supposed to make anything of her life but who has somehow overcome the odds. My position is a role model, a leader and a guide. I am responsible for the gifts I've been given and to use them to better society as much as is possible. I am limited only by what I allow to limit me; as Ayn Rand said "the question is not who will let me, but who will stop me".

That class further solidified my commitment to living a new way; I now knew how to access my higher wisdom and had identified some of the limiting beliefs I'd internalized from my family of origin. I realized how deeply ingrained those beliefs had become and how much they orchestrated my life, unconsciously. As

I made them conscious, I was able to choose to live differently.

When I opened to the flow of the Universe, things began to happen that I couldn't have imagined before. Battles that had been going on for years were suddenly resolved. I fostered wonderful relationships with new friends and colleagues, and quickly began to rise in leadership in my university. I was invited to speak at conferences; flown out to corporate retreats and was soon offered a job in California. Although it took a while to get the pieces in place, I could see our lives unfolding in a new way. I couldn't be more excited.

Reconstruction

Although I hadn't yet named it, what I was experiencing was something called Post Traumatic Growth[4]. As the name suggests, Post Traumatic Growth is when a person who has gone through a

---

[4] Tedeschi, R., & Calhoun, L. (2004). Posttraumatic [sic] growth: Conceptual foundations and empirical evidence. *Psychological Inquiry, 15*(1), 1–18.

significant trauma is transformed in the process and rewrites their mental schemas. Irv Yalom[5], noted existential psychiatrist, wrote, "A confrontation with death arouses anxiety but also has the potential of vastly enriching life . . . [as it can serve to] awaken consciousness". Wong[6] suggested the terror of death could be overcome with a passion for life and a zest for living, by facing adversity with courage, heroism, and a "defiant human spirit [that can be] destroyed but not defeated". The transformational potential of trauma, death anxiety, and sorrow is found in the midst of the suffering. Taylor[7] suggested,

---

[5] Yalom, I. (1980). *Existential psychotherapy*. New York, NY: Basic Books.

[6] Wong, P. T. P. (2009). *Positive existential psychotherapy and pathways to death acceptance: A review of staring at the sun: Overcoming the terror of death.* San Francisco, CA: PsychCritiques.

[7] Taylor, S. (2012). Transformation through suffering: A study of individuals who have experienced positive psychological transformation following

When stress and anxiety are constant over a long period and build up to a high enough intensity, the psyche may dissolve. The pressure becomes so intense that the structure cannot maintain itself. In most cases, this equates with a psychotic break—the collapse of the psyche leaves a vacuum, and the person feels defenseless and emotionally unstable, unable to cope. But for a few individuals, this is not a breakdown but a "breakup"—a new self emerges into the vacuum. Another, latent self-system—or psychological structure—unfolds and establishes itself, almost like a butterfly emerging from a caterpillar larva. (p. 45)

Taylor explained, "The main reason turmoil and trauma can trigger transformation is because they have the effect of dissolving psychological attachments" (p. 45). The falling away of these attachments, the psychological scaffolding, results in the loss of one's sense of self and identity. Taylor stated, "The person feels naked and lost . . . but at this very point, he or she

---

periods of intense turmoil. *Journal of Humanistic Psychology, 52*(1), 30–52.

is, paradoxically, close to a state of liberation". It is, as pointed out by my colleague, Sandy Sela-Smith, "Everything you thought you were falls away so who you really are can emerge." Sandy suggested that what most of people identify that themselves or their personality is a false self that is constructed and reconstructed over one's lifetime as a protective mask to be accepted or to feel safe in the world, and in time, people come to believe the false self is who they really are.

My own psychological scaffolding had come tumbling down around me in the previous years; my beliefs about everything had been challenged and I was forced to my knees. In the process, I had to learn how to live again in a different way and instead of unconsciously living out beliefs and agreements I'd made in years past, I was facing the Herculean task of consciously recreating my life and beliefs in a way that served the new woman I'd become. I was like a newborn deer, taking wobbly and tentative steps, not yet strong enough to run but learning how to stand again.

A New Beginning

I sold as many of my belongings as I could, keeping only those things that were necessary and those that were irreplaceable. I packed up what was left, donated the rest and loaded up a U-Haul. My children and I were headed to California where I had been offered a position in a psychological training institute that was founded and led by some of my heroes in psychology.

After months of preparation and laying the groundwork to go, I was finally ready to head out. I was driving out alone to a small island town in the San Francisco Bay area with a small U-Haul attached to my car. I would drive straight through, only stopping to get gas, eat and sleep. It was a 19-hour road trip, and with stops, I figured it would take me at least 24 hours to arrive. I was planning to leave on Tuesday morning but as things sometimes happen, my plans were delayed. I left the Denver area at about 1 p.m., 5 hours after I planned to leave and drove through the familiar highways with a sense of relief.

This city, once my home, now had become a cauldron of painful memories. I drove past landmarks that had the taint of sadness attached to them. Denver, in spite of its beauty, had become a prison to me.

Leaving to CA, albeit for a job and further training, was really about getting away from Colorado and starting over. Here, I was stunted and trapped and my soul needed freedom to soar.

As the miles ticked off behind me, my spirits soared. The future was a blank page and I couldn't wait to see what would come. The mountains passed behind me and I finally stopped after 9 hours of driving to sleep. I pulled into a truck stop, parked next to the long haul trucks, and climbed in the back of my SUV and snuggled up to sleep. Surprisingly, I fell asleep quickly and woke only a few hours later and was ready to hit the road again. I went inside to freshen up and get some coffee. Soon, I was getting back on the highway. It was dark as it was the early morning hours but I sipped my coffee, and cranked up the music for the next leg of the journey.

The sun came up as I was driving through the salt plains of Utah. It was stunning to see the white contrast with the red rocks of Utah. There were messages and images left throughout the sand in rocks by passersby. One message said simply, "one love" and had a peace sign. I felt love and gratitude flowing through my body---grateful for the future that was unfolding before me and love for the new life I was creating.

When I crossed into California, I shouted with joy. Soon, I noticed the elevation began to lower and I knew I was almost there. I arrived in the San Francisco Bay area shortly after 3 p.m. I was exhausted but still had work to be done. I parked my car and the U-Haul and walked the two blocks to the property management company with whom I had leased my home. I got my keys, some coffee and went back to the house. The home I'd rented was the only one I could find that had the space I needed and allowed dogs. It looked like a barn and didn't have a functioning garage, yard or parking space. It was dusty and musty, the windowsills were rotting wood, there were no screens and the appliances were ancient.

It was perfect.

❖

The next two days were a whirlwind. After the U-Haul was unloaded, I hit the local Target and purchased the essentials we'd need in our new home. I opened the windows, unpacked, unloaded and put some music on the speaker as I danced around happily. I found a local furniture store, and when I arrived, found exactly what we needed to get started. To my surprise and joy, they store offered same day delivery and set up so I raced home to be there when they arrived. Soon, the home that was empty only 24 hours earlier was clean, filled with furniture, and boxes were unpacked. I found an appliance store that delivered my new (used) washer and dryer and set it up. I was a woman on a mission; I wanted the children to arrive to a home, so I unpacked their room first. I carefully hung up their clothes, set out their toys and made sure their beds were made with their favorite toys. On the second night in the house, I slept in my new bed on brand new sheets and pillows. The towels were hung, the refrigerator full and clothes put away. I was ready for my babies to arrive.

Their flight landed early Friday morning. I was so excited to pick them up that I was awake with the sun. I headed to Oakland International Airport, using my trusty GPS because I'd only ever been in this town once before and had no idea where I was going. When they arrived, we raced back home and they got to see their new home. We took the dogs for a walk, grabbed lunch and headed to the beach. They caught their first glimpse of San Francisco across the bay. Feeling the sand under my toes, and the wind whipping my hair while I watched my babies laugh and play in the water was the freest I'd felt in ages.

❖

It turns out that it wasn't that simple. Leaving a place physically and leaving it emotionally are not quite the same. With some distance and perspective, I was able to see some things differently and much clearer. There is a saying that "wherever you go, there you are" and that was true in this case. Although I'd done some work, and broken through some beliefs, there was more to be done.

We were away from the drama and turmoil that had engulfed our lives for the last four years and we began to rebuild. The children and I settled into our new community quickly and easily. We met friends, found a favorite coffee shop, joined a new gym and began exploring the area. We rode our bikes almost everywhere and spent our weekends either at the beach, in San Francisco or at the nearest Six Flags. Things were beginning to look up for us.

It was about this time that I began to realize how just how much stress I'd been under. When things became peaceful, it was a stark contrast to the lack of calm I'd felt before. Things weren't perfect in California but they were simple. We had a routine, we had structure, and we had adventure, fun and mostly...peace.

Yet, I was still a work in progress. I knew it was time to shed another layer and step into the next phase.

I first met the man who would become my therapist a couple of years before at a psychology conference. He was my psychology idol—I read one of his books in my master's program and it transformed my course of learning. I'd followed his work for years and in March 2013, I was able to meet him for the first time. It was one of the highlights of my life.

After I moved to the Bay Area, where he had an office, I had an impulse to reach out to him to see if he was accepting new clients. In a stroke of fate, he was and I jumped at the chance to work with him. On the day of our first appointment, I drove into the city, crossing the Bay Bridge with something bigger than butterflies in my stomach.

Driving in San Francisco is a unique experience. The hills and steep streets are extreme and sometimes unexpected. Every time I'd go into the city, I'd get anxious. Those steep hills made me feel like my car would tip over backwards which is, of course, completely irrational. In fact, once when Gabriel and Eden and I were going to a concert at Golden Gate

Park, I turned a corner onto an extremely steep hill; I was so nervous that the kids were laughing at me and Gabriel chortled, "Oh my God, mom is FREAKING OUT".

The thing with anxiety is that it is not like fear. Fear is usually tied to something tangible or rational. When fear arises, it's generally because there is something to actually fear. In this case, with the steep streets, it wasn't rational. Logically, I knew that there was no way I was going to tip over or get stuck but emotionally, every time I'd turn onto a steep street, I would feel the panic hit my entire body. My palms would sweat. My stomach would knot up and my throat would tighten. Then, my mind would try to calm my body and my body would completely reject all reason. This entire war would wage inside of me until I reached the top of the hill. It was, as you can imagine, simply *delightful*.

The steep street anxiety was a nice distraction from the anxiety I was feeling about going to work with my psychology idol in therapy. Going to therapy is challenging enough—there is such a stigma attached to it that even though I am a therapist and know how important therapy is, there was still a part of me that felt embarrassed. I felt like I should be better than I was—further along in my life and emotional state than I was.

Deep inside, I felt that I was actually maybe broken. I wondered if he would see through my façade, find me irreparable and declare me a fraud.

My first session, I left Alameda early and arrived in Russian Hill about 15 minutes before my scheduled time and as fate would have it, his office was located right at the top of one of those big hilly streets. There was no way I could avoid the anxiety that hit me as I traversed those hills and navigated into a parking spot. A few moments of breathing slightly calmed me but I was still nervous about meeting with him. I finally got out of the car and began walking to the office. It was a gorgeous day and I could see the ocean for miles, stretching beyond my vision. There is something about gazing at the ocean that makes me feel small and insignificant. It's as if the vastness of the ocean is telling me to keep things in perspective. I felt the tight grip on my emotions relax further.

I went in, pressed the call button and soon, heard his voice over the intercom. I announced myself, and he came to meet me. It felt like small bats had taken residence in my stomach and were flying around within me. My heart was racing and my body temperature was rising. The excitement and anxiety curled up in my body like two snakes intertwined; I simply couldn't tell which was which.

He arrived in the lobby and greeted me. I was much more formal than he was, addressing him with his title. He is much smaller than the giant I'd built him to be in my mind. I imagined him larger than life before I met him and he was still up on a pedestal. I was still struck by the fact that he's not very tall, older and his hands show age spots. He is very much human and it is both comforting and disconcerting.

In his office, we sit and I explain that I am nervous to work with him because I have him on such a pedestal. He laughs and says, "Well, we'll have to fix that" and my anxiety goes a little lower. He asks me why I'm here, and why I sought him out and I start out intellectually, describing my life in a somewhat detached way. I told him how my whole life had fallen apart between 2006 and 2010 and the whole time, I knew I was avoiding saying what really concerned me. I looked in his eyes and saw compassion there and it was as if the compassion was a hammer, breaking through my defenses.

Tears welled up in my eyes and began to flow down my face and I finally said the truth of why I sought him out. I said, "My son has a heart condition and I am scared he's going to die. I don't think I can handle that". As I said it, my voice cracked and the simple act of me voicing that to another person broke me even further. Uncontrollable tears burst out of me and my body began to shake, sobs wracking my whole frame. I cried for a few moments as he sat quietly, making comforting sounds and witnessing my internal struggle.

I finally gathered myself and felt more composed. He said, "Well, I agree that you're a good candidate for psychotherapy" but what I heard was "wow, you are totally messed up because if HE thinks you need therapy, you must really be in bad shape". I noted the discrepancy between what he said and what I heard but I didn't mention it to him then. I left the session feeling raw and vulnerable but somewhat relived for having pushed myself to be honest about the thing that scared me the most.

Although I'd been aware of Gabriel having what could be a life limiting illness, I'd never given it much deep thought. I simply couldn't go there in my mind. I'd kept my fears at bay and took refuge from the other heart transplant recipients around me. There was Brittney, who I met shortly after Gabriel's transplant who was then a teenager and was doing fine. There was Connor, who was a two-time transplant recipient, a thriving teen when we met and had since become a college student and ghost hunter. I imagined Gabriel on the same path and never let myself consider the other possibility, which were all the parents I'd known over the years who weren't so fortunate.

Truthfully, I avoided thinking about the other possibility because it was too painful. Every time the idea of Gabriel not making it came to my mind, I dropped it like a hot potato. It was not something I would allow to linger in my mind. I told myself that I was just "thinking positive" and being a woman of faith but I knew on some level that I was avoiding facing the reality.

I began working with my therapist weekly. Each week, I would drive into the City and up those big hills. I'd gaze over the water, take a deep breath and plunge into the depths of my soul with this trusted guide. Each week, he would ask me about my son, "what is his prognosis" and each week, I'd give him the same answer, "no one really knows because of the changes and advances in medicine". The truth was that I'd never actually asked Gabriel's doctors what his prognosis was because I didn't want to know. If I looked at the data or across research trends, I could make myself believe that Gabriel would be one of the outliers but if I actually asked the doctors, I'd know concrete information. Concrete answers would mean I'd have to shed my fantasies and hopes to face reality. I wasn't sure I wanted to do that.

There is a certain measure of comfort in not knowing which is why people say that ignorance is bliss. The truth had often, in my experience, served as an executioner of hope. The truth of my husband's behavior, when I finally accepted it, was the executioner's axe swinging at the hopes I'd held onto for a family unit. The truth of my family dynamics killed my hopes that I would ever be accepted or embraced in that environment and still be able to be honest and authentic. The truth does set one free but it comes with a price. I wasn't sure I was ready or even willing to pay this toll.

Gabriel had a heart clinic appointment sometime in the third month after I started therapy. We left in the early morning hours to arrive on time and drove quietly. The appointment went as it usually does, with blood draws, echocardiogram and an EKG (electrocardiogram). After all the testing is complete, we wait to meet with the Heart Transplant Coordinator, the nurse who is tasked with monitoring the transplant patient care and the Cardiologist who manages the care. By the time they arrived in our room, Gabriel and Eden were both tired and grumpy and I was exhausted. Gabriel was examined and finally set free to have a snack and play with Eden.

The doctor looked at me and said, "we aren't terribly concerned about this now but we wanted to let you know that Gabriel's blood shows some levels of donor specific antibodies which could be an early warning sign of rejection. We aren't too concerned about it now because the levels are low but we will keep an eye on it".

I felt the floor fall away from me but I managed to stay calm. I asked some questions about what it meant and if there was anything I should watch for and they were both reassuring that there was nothing I could do other than keep brining him in for his appointments and to make sure he gets his meds on time.

The time seemed right to ask the question I'd been avoiding. My voice was strained but pushed through the vocal cords and I heard my own voice ask, "What is Gabriel's prognosis?" The doctor looked at me and said, "'If he continues to do well, we think he will make it to his teen years or early adult but the odds are that he will eventually go into heart failure and will need another transplant. If at that time, we can't find a donor, he won't survive". I stood there, stunned, hearing my children playing together and tears flooded down my cheeks. I asked more questions, hoping against hope that there would be another answer that would come. None did.

The appointment was over and so I gathered my children and our belongings to make our way back to our car. The children were tired and had no idea that I was in turmoil as I buckled them safely into their seats. We drove off of the hospital campus and they both fell asleep. As the quiet descended in the car, the pain rose again in my chest and tears began rolling down my cheeks. I grabbed my phone and texted my friend Tony, and told him what I'd learned. His response was immediate and he said, "Oh my god, I'm so sorry. Are you ok?" I replied, "No, I am a mess".

That was an understatement but I didn't know how to describe what I was feeling. I looked in the rearview mirror at Gabriel and Eden, both sleeping peacefully and waves of pain washed over me. I couldn't begin to name the depth of the despair that I was feeling. How could I ever come to terms with this? How would I be ok if the worst happened? Would I survive?

The drive home took some time and I gathered myself along the way. As the miles ticked off behind me, the worse scenario began to play in my mind. I imagined the worst; going in for an appointment and hearing the words "rejection" coming from the doctor. In my mind, I saw Gabriel lying in a hospital bed, fading away and I saw Eden helplessly standing by. I saw myself lying in the bed with him, holding him as life slipped away from him, begging him not to leave us. Tears burned my eyes and I wiped them away.

I wondered if I was a match to Gabriel and if I were, how I could orchestrate a situation where I gave him my own heart. Then, I wondered if that were to happen, what would happen to my children. Would Eden understand if I gave my own life to save her brother? Would both children feel abandoned if I were somehow able to do that?

I saw the funeral in my mind. I saw myself, fragile and wounded, holding myself together to be strong for my daughter. I felt the weight that comes from empty arms that ache for the presence of a child who would never come home. I felt the emptiness that would fill my heart for the rest of my life. I wondered if I would survive such an event or if I would simply give up on life, and become a chain smoking alcoholic who spent my days lying in a bed of despair.

It was then that I realized that giving up, even in the face of the worst pain imaginable was never an option because I had two lives depending on me. If we lost Gabriel, Eden would only have me remaining and for me to give up on life would be to give up on her. I knew I couldn't do that to her. The last time I'd thought deeply about Gabriel dying, I wanted to drive off a cliff and to end my own life as well. Now, I noticed, I didn't want to die anymore. I wanted to live.

I began to talk more openly with my therapist and my friends about my fears for Gabriel's life. Tears came easily and more frequently when I spoke of my concerns. I felt myself touching into that deeper pain and letting it be known, and allowing others to help me carry the weight. It wasn't easy to share my feelings, and sometimes, those feelings would come bursting out at inappropriate times. That happened mostly because although I was talking about it more, I still wasn't fully feeling it. I'd managed to distract myself from the pain by throwing myself into work, into my academic pursuits and in an unhealthy relationship.

The two most significant times I can remember having emotional outbursts were both fueled by alcohol. The first time, someone asked me, after shots of tequila, how my dissertation research was going and I immediately burst into sobs. I cried and said how terrified I was and how much fear I had. The second time was at a professional football game with my brother, also fueled by alcohol. Gabriel was at the same game and was delighting in the sounds, energy and fun he was having. I, on the other hand, was seeing the light in his eyes and feeling the pain of wondering how many times I'd see that in him. I wondered how many times I would enjoy his laughter, his hugs and his kisses. I told my brother that I was terrified of losing him and immediately burst into tears. I was angry with him because I wanted him to be more supportive and I lashed out at him. He, in turn, lashed back and we left the game angry and hurt. The next day, sober, we talked and began to repair our relationship on a more honest level. The pain we'd both been avoiding had made itself known and now that it was out, there was no more avoiding it.

I realized then that I had two choices; I could continue avoiding the pain and risk having it come out in untimely unconscious ways or I could deal with it directly. Although I wanted to avoid it, I knew that if I were to ever truly overcome it, I would have to face it.

Joseph Campbell, mythologist and psychologist said once "if you are falling, dive" and I did just that. I did what I had been avoiding and intentionally went into my pain. I leaned into it. I made myself sit with my own discomfort instead of moving away from it. When the grief would come up, I would let it be present and I would sit with it. I went back and read my journals from when Gabriel was an infant. I watched the videos that were taken by the news station and I saw myself in them, so young and wounded, and as I watched them, allowed whatever feelings showed up to be present. I stopped avoiding my pain and instead, embraced it. It was terrifying because I had no idea what was on the other side of the abyss I was leaping into, or if there was another side. Perhaps, there was only pain and that would be the mantle I would march under for the rest of my life. I had no way of knowing.

Oddly, I soon began to feel lighter and freer. It wasn't as though thinking of Gabriel's death gave me any relief but rather, that I began to understand that by avoiding the idea of it, I was only holding the pain closer. The more I avoided it, the more it wanted to be known. The feelings were there, and they weren't going to magically disappear just because I didn't want to feel them. They were going to continue to be there until I dealt with them. As I had often said to my own clients, the only way through was by going through.

I committed to the leap. I felt myself changing slowly and began to feel more grounded, more peaceful and stronger. I hated the thought of losing Gabriel and yet, I realized that even if the worst were to come, I'd make it through.

One night, I received notice that a close friend of mine from childhood had suddenly died. I was in

California and unable to fly to Colorado for his services and I was on my own with my pain. The next morning, I packed a lunch, the kids and some blankets. We got ready and loaded up and headed to the safest place I could think to go; the beach.

We arrived at Stinson beach in the late morning. The sun was shining on the waves, and for as far as I could see was water. I set up camp and the kids were off to play in the water. I stayed nearby, watching them play and with the cool water lapping at my toes, my feet buried in the sand, I felt the grief from the loss of my friend wash over me. Tears rolled down my cheeks and fell into the ocean water at my feet. The sun's warm rays embraced me, like a hug from a loved one and staring out into the horizon where the ocean seemed endless, I felt tiny. As my tears blended into the water and washed away from the shore, I felt the pain gripping my heart releasing and soon, the grief wasn't so heavy. I wept for my friend, and for his family. I wept for our friends who were also so sad. Eventually, I moved back to the blanket and pulled out my journal. A poem burst out of me; a tribute to his life and to the journey he'd led. I said a prayer and released him into the hands of the Divine. With a deep breath, I exhaled the pain of death and inhaled the joy of life. Finished writing, I jumped up and went to my children. We spent the remainder of the day laughing, building sand castles and enjoying life.

The ocean waters healed me that day, as they taught me that while our lives may seem big, they are only a small part of the greater whole. As my tears became one with the ocean, so does any life become one with the whole of humanity. The sand castles we built that day have long washed into the ocean and only remain a memory. Someday, my life will wash away and I, too, will only be a memory. My children, parents, pets, friends and loved ones will all become one with the ocean as well. The only thing that is guaranteed in this life we live is that it is temporary. Whatever "this" might be; whether it is joy, pain, bliss or terror...well, this too, shall pass.

It always does.

A happy accident

I stopped doing intense physical exercise and started to practice yoga because I realized that my mind was always in the frame of competition and pushing harder when I did other workouts. On some level, I realized that what I most needed was not more driven and compulsive behaviors but to slow down and be gentler with myself.

I'd done yoga before and enjoyed it but as with all things, I approached it from a place of being the best, and of competition. There was no mindfulness, awareness or simply allowing myself to be where I was with it in the past. I'd missed the whole point.

Now, I began to approach yoga as it ought to be approached, mindfully, and gently. I began to tune into my body and listen to what my body was saying. If I felt the need to drop into child's pose, I would do it and breathe through my concerns that someone might judge me for it. I began to realize that no one in my classes cared what I was doing or not doing and that the narrative I was constructing about others judgment was simply an outward projection of the judgment I levied at myself.

It was on my mat that I began to loosen up and open my heart in deeper ways. I found myself being aware and conscious of my inner dialogue, which wasn't very kind. I found myself comparing myself and always coming up short. The ability to release, let go and just breathe was foreign to me and it was a challenge to simply learn to be.

My first serious savasana, or corpse pose, was tragically amusing. It was tragic because it showed me just how far away from relaxation and mindfulness I'd gotten. After a particularly rigorous vinyassa class, the instructor encouraged us to lie back and to allow our feet to fall open naturally. The point of savasana is to surrender and to be supported on the Earth, effortlessly. It is a process of going within, being within and allowing oneself to relax fully while remaining aware. It is all about conscious relaxation and releasing tension. It highlights the areas where one might hold tension and anxiety and although it looks easy, it is incredibly challenging.

When it was time to lie back, I complied and took about two breaths before my eyes popped open and anxiety began to rise within me. I simply couldn't relax and my mind was off to the races. I began rehearsing my to do list, and it was all I could to do remain still and lying on the floor. I really wanted to get up and bolt out of the room. Fortunately, I didn't do that but I did become aware of how hard it was for me to relax. This time, I didn't judge myself but rather, was able to approach it from a place of curiosity and interest and a slight bit of humor.

Although I'd dabbled in meditation and mindfulness up to this point, this yoga class was a significant turning point for me. I realized how hard even sitting still is for me...how I've always distracted myself with books, thinking, music or doing something. The idea of sitting quietly without any distraction was scary and anxiety provoking that I knew I must start immediately. Part of my commitment to learning to live deeply was to start doing something every day that scared me. This seemed like a great place to start.

I began by walking on the beach without my phone on, or headphones in. I would listen to the water, the birds and the sounds of nature and resist the urge to grab my phone and check social media. I started sitting quietly and listening to my breath more often and within a few moments, would find anxiety creeping in and tapping on my shoulder, reminding me of all the things I needed to be doing. Being mindful was hard work—harder than I'd anticipated. For someone who was driven, simply learning to just be was one of the biggest challenges I faced.

Determined, I continued to practice yoga a few times a week and mindfulness daily. I learned how to breathe through the positions I felt most uncomfortable with in yoga class and learned how to allow myself the room to push a little further than I was comfortable with and not go so far that I was hurt. I learned to embrace the challenge without engaging in the struggle as I began to understand that struggle is indeed a choice. That may sound crazy to many but struggle is a decision, just like suffering is a decision. The reality of life is that pain and challenges come to anyone who dares to live. Even those who are most sheltered in their lives will face challenges. It is part of the nature of being alive but not everyone who faces challenges will suffer. Only those who choose the path of suffering will suffer; the others will experience challenge as nothing more than an opportunity to grow.

Soon, I began to realize that yoga has a subversive agenda and that is to transform the lives of its practitioners. When I engaged with yoga, I discovered that the same ability to breathe through painful poses carried over into my daily life. Circumstances and issues that used to be a huge trigger for me and would send me into an emotional spiral lost their power over me. It was, as Bob Ross used to say, a very happy accident. I went into yoga to tighten my ass but as Eric Pasekl noted, it was all about getting my head out of my ass. I noticed this most clearly when I received a call that Gabriel's Social Security Disability Insurance (SSDI) may be cancelled and I was able to pause, breathe and consciously choose my response instead of my normal reaction.

A state of emergency

One of the horrors that parents of children with CHD face is the nightmare that is healthcare in the USA. Before Gabriel's diagnosis, I'd never even much considered healthcare and as a healthy, vital young woman, didn't much care. That changed after his diagnosis because suddenly, my unborn child had a pre-existing condition that made him untouchable in the insurance realm.

Gabriel received emergency state insurance for the first couple of years after he was born and then I enrolled him in a program offered by an insurance company that helps families who make too much money for state insurance but can't afford private insurance. With Gabriel's heart condition, there was simply no way I could afford insurance; one visit alone was nearly $40,000 and he had those four times a year when he's healthy. Add in medications, sickness, other visits and larger procedures and the cost for his care alone is well over $200,000.

After years of applying, gathering paperwork and sitting through meetings and hearings, I finally got Gabriel enrolled on SSDI. I thought it was a Godsend but quickly learned that it was more of a nightmare than anything else. Although Gabriel now had insurance, it was tied to my income and any changes in income could impact his insurance. Over the course of a couple of years, he lost his insurance a handful of times and I had to fight to get it back; they seemed not to care that a kid with CHD who didn't have insurance was at risk of serious harm and absolutely needed his medication. They would yank insurance with little notice, which would require me to spend hours and hours resolving the issue. Fortunately, each time I was able to get it fixed when it happened but it came at a high price emotionally and was a huge drain on time.

This happened once after we moved to Alameda and about two months after I began diligently practicing yoga and mindfulness. Instead of my normal response, I was able to detach from the emotion and handle it calmly. It was, to me, nothing short of a miracle.

Unfortunately, this wouldn't be the last time the insurance was yanked out from under us and it wasn't the last time I'd be challenged to find a solution to a big problem in a short time. It was apparent that insurance companies weren't friendly to those with pre-existing conditions, and the government supported programs necessitated an income so low that a family of three couldn't survive. I realized that we would have to find another way.

❖

Soon after, I had a striking realization. I became aware that my decision to go forward in my life and to choose to live, no matter what, wasn't based on me. It was based on my children and what I thought they needed. I discovered that my intense focus on Gabriel and his life was real, but it also served a purpose for me. By channeling all of my fears about death into his life and medical issues, I'd been able to avoid facing MY life and the decisions I made. By remaining stuck in the terror, I'd missed the awe of living.

I'd long been a driven woman, always striving for the next accomplishment or to complete the next task. I was relentless toward myself, holding an impossible standard and mercilessly driving toward some perceived desired end. I was alive but not living.

That realization drove me to examine my life in a deeper way. Instead of imagining Gabriel's life ending, I imagined my life ending. I closed my eyes and imagined that I was dead and that there was a funeral for me. I wondered who would come, and what would be the legacy I would leave, if any. I wrote in my journal:

But Gabriel's diagnosis has also been a diversion from my own death anxiety. If I am only focused on HIM, and making his dreams come true and making sure he has a life worth remembering, I am effectively cutting off my own experience of death anxiety. I am not afraid of my own death because I don't think about it. I think about Gabriel's death and whether I'll eventually bury him and that is so huge that I rarely think about my own.

Last week, though, it struck me. My own terror of death hit me like a freight train. Looking at my life, my choices, where I am now and where I want to be reduced me to tears.

If I were to die today, what legacy would remain?

"Here lies Lisa Vallejos. She was a 36-year-old divorced mother of two who was pursuing a PhD. Too often, Lisa allowed school to become her primary focus, and neglected the truly important things in life. Lisa was most often a great mother but had many moments of impatience and frustration with her children, which were mostly misdirected. Lisa was single, and often lonely, because she was

focused on other areas of her life. Lisa really wanted to fall in love and share her life with someone but she never did because she was too consumed with other pursuits. Lisa's academic career was moderately successful but she knew she had more to give than she did. Lisa was estranged from her family, had a tense relationship with her mother and her brother had become more of a stranger than a sibling. Despite her large extended family, Lisa was virtually alone. Lisa's intimate relationships were intense and short-lived, and she tended to be attracted to emotionally unavailable men. Lisa was in debt, overweight, lonely and often unhappy with her life choices, as she spent much of her energy focusing on the future and her children. Lisa died feeling that she was wasting her life, waiting to be finished with school so she could begin living."

As I write this, a few things come up for me. The first is a remarkable sense of astonishment at how hard I am on myself, and the second is a sense of regret for my choices up to now. I do not regret going to graduate school, but I do regret some of how I've handled it.

If I were to re-write my death announcement to what I want it to be, here's what it would say:

"Here lies Lisa Vallejos. Lisa was a dynamic, vibrant woman who lived life with a fullness that was liberating to many. Lisa was a woman who faced the challenges that life presented, and instead of bowing under the pressure, rose to the occasion. Lisa lived life with an open heart, open mind, and with a deep sense of awe and reverence for the experience of living. Lisa's children remember her as being the best mother ever, as she worked hard to provide them with both a sense of security and adventure. Lisa's children learned a solid work ethic, great financial management skills, and most importantly, how to truly live.

Lisa leaves behind a family that adores her, clients whose lives have been forever changed, friends who cherish her, an academic community that will forever feel her absence."

I realized as I wrote that, that there is a gap from where I am and where I want to be...and only I can change that.

Reconstruction

The gap between who I'd been before everything fell apart and who I was becoming since was closing. The Lisa who was here before that diagnosis was gone, and she wasn't coming back. The new version of me was far wiser and knew far too much to go back to an unconscious way of living. The intervening years were a process of me letting go of who I used to be and trying to figure out who I was now.

Whereas many cling to possessions and physical comforts during times of change, I found that those very things became increasingly restrictive. I no longer wanted the big house, the nice car, and the white picket fence as much as I desired freedom. This freedom I sought was not a shedding of responsibilities but rather a renewed focus on what truly mattered and a realignment of my goals to fit my priorities. No longer was I driven by the desire for material comforts drive me but instead my desire for interpersonal and intrapersonal expressiveness came to the forefront. My mantra became, "If it doesn't contribute to my joy, I won't do it." That belief extended to all areas of my life. Whereas I once felt driven to complete my doctoral degree, I no longer felt compelled to do so and instead became re-engaged with my love of learning. When I shifted from terror to awe, my work changed.

Suddenly, I was able to sit to read and write for long stretches of time because I was motivated by passion instead of driven by the need to fill a hole in my life. Physically, this change manifested in my levels of physical activity and dietary lifestyle as well. No longer was the desire to exercise out of obligation but arose instead from a sense of deep gratitude for a healthy body, which allowed me to move. My awe and reverence for life changed the way I took care of my physical body and the attention I gave to self-care and nurturing.

My desires were no longer about being the best at everything but were about living well. I wasn't quite sure what that meant yet, but I knew I was on my way to finding out. I became more calm, grounded and mindful in my daily life. I felt in control of myself, without being rigid. My relationship with my children deepened, and I cultivated meaningful friendships. I stopped being a slave to my time and schedule, and began to learn how to have fun again.

One day, leaving a luncheon, I caught a glimpse of a woman in the mirror coming toward me and I recognized her as a friend. My face lit up with a delighted smile and I moved toward her. Only then did I realize that I'd simply caught my own reflection in a large mirror and that realization touched me deeply.

Once, as a child, I'd done the same in a department store, running toward my own reflection after having seen a friend to play with. Now, 30 some years later, I finally saw myself as a friend again.

One morning, my family attended a volunteer appreciation event for the regional organ donation organization. At this event, a family spoke whose daughter had recently received a heart transplant. The family had made a video of the daughter's time in the hospital to document their journey. A nurse in the video said to the child, "Don't ever give your parents a hard time because they have been through so much and love you more than you will ever know." Hearing that, I felt as if I had been hit in the chest with a sledgehammer as a flood of memories rushed through my mind; the times I swallowed back my fear to be brave for Gabriel; the times I would leave his side and weep in my mother's lap; the times that I wished I could change places with him; the times that I raged internally at being powerless to prevent his pain; the times I had to hold him down when he was terrified of a medical procedure and how hard it was to see him suffering. In a rush of unexpected and powerful tears, I felt the pain I had swallowed for so many years. I saw my own experience reflected in the eyes of that mother and felt a surge of compassion for myself. For a moment, I saw myself as a wounded warrior who bravely marches on. The high expectations I set for myself ceased along with the unrelenting drive to do more, be more, and become more.

I offered to myself the gift I had offered others countless times: the space to grieve. I sat at that table with the 28-year-old version of me, who was young and terrified, watching her child being poked, turning blue, and struggling just to stay warm. I sat with myself, the new mother of a 13-day-old infant who released her baby to the care of the skilled surgeons and walked away, not knowing whether I would ever see him again. I sat with the version of me that saw my son's newly transplanted heart beating in his terribly swollen body that did not feel fear but hope. I sat with myself, at my varying ages, when I sat with my son as he was sedated, his eyes growing heavy as he stared into mine. I cried, unashamed and boldly, without feeling the need to apologize, or the desire to run from the room. I sat with myself, wrapping myself with love and kindness and offered to those very wounded, yet very strong parts of myself the space to simply be. There was nothing I needed to do, nothing I needed to fix, and there was nothing wrong with how I felt along the way. I was one step closer to being my own friend again.

      As part of the journey, I decided to do my doctoral research on the experience of being a parent with a child who has a life limiting congenital heart defect. I was genuinely curious about the experience of others and what I noticed along the way was that there didn't seem to be much support available. I understood that to a degree; children's hospitals are there to treat the kids, not the parents. Intuitively, however, I knew that if parents weren't coping well, the kids would struggle as well. During my research, I learned that things like anticipatory grief, or the experience of feeling grief for a loss that one anticipates, is normal and that many parents with chronically ill children feel that way. I learned that survivor guilt for people who are transplant recipients is also normal. I learned that there is a thing called "chronic sorrow" which is ongoing, cyclical pain for those whose lives have ongoing loss that has no predicable end in sight. I learned that parents often endure extreme situations, and are often required to make major life decisions under extreme stress. I also learned that within extreme trauma, there are the seeds of potential and that when everything falls apart, it can be the sign of a new beginning.

Contingency of life

Life with a chronically ill kid exposes parents to turmoil. The diagnosis, treatment and management of the illness are all unpredictable and life-changing events. The path that one is on before the diagnosis will change dramatically. Suddenly, one's life must be built around precautions, doctor's appointments, follow-ups, medication administration, and sudden illnesses. In the time since Gabriel's diagnosis, he's had three bouts of pneumonia, one of which necessitated an overnight hospital stay. When that happens, our lives take a sudden swerve and suddenly, anything on the agenda must be changed around. It takes a measure of flexibility to manage these sudden changes in life plans.

To accept that life is fundamentally dynamic was quite challenging. I had taken the position, as a young girl, that I would not be vulnerable. To accept and embrace that vulnerability as an adult as the price of fully living was very challenging. Before Gabriel's diagnosis, I lived my life in a very structured way. I'd make plans, work the plan and achieve my goals. I lacked spontaneity and was extremely rigid in my thinking, ways of being and how I saw the world. There was only black and white, good and bad, right or wrong. To learn to embrace the subtleties and nuances of living was quite challenging. In college, I actually had my closet color coded and lived in a house so spotless it was almost a museum. There was no room for clutter or mess because I wanted my life to be perfect. There was no way that I could continue living that way after Gabriel's diagnosis and I had to learn how to let loose with my grip and desire to control my environment, and my life.

I took tentative steps: not planning every minute of every day, skipping housework to go to the park, and letting myself sit on the beach for hours and resting instead of tackling my to-do list. I accepted that where I am today may not be where I will be tomorrow; things can change instantly, and although it seems a very scary place to be, it has been most liberating. Before I felt that security was a priority; however, I have come to realize that freedom is far more valuable. Part of one's being free is the willingness to accept the change that could come at any time and knowing that whatever comes, I will be fine. I had to trust myself to be able to manage whatever curve ball life might throw my way.

Embracing this meant I also had to embrace something else; that life is contingent and that the rain and sun fall on the heads of the righteous and unrighteous just the same. I can do everything right and still not have the desired outcome because there are factors that are beyond my control. No one has any more right than anyone else to be here, and every moment one is offered is a gift that can be taken at any time. I came to understand that ground I had built my life upon was really unstable, unsure, and can be pulled out at any time. My efforts to build security or to control the environment were a futile attempt to diffuse the feelings of being completely powerless over the major events of my life.

Spiritual awakening

Part of this journey for me was a spiritual awakening, as the structures of religion I'd held before could no longer support what I was experiencing. A significant aspect of my spiritual transformation has been in my taking back responsibility for my life. No longer do I feel at the mercy of god. Instead, I recognize that I alone am responsible for my life. Although there may be circumstances that present that are out of my control, I am fully in control of how I respond.

As a Christian, I was always looking to be the bible to tell me how to behave; it was my way to measure my behavior against the biblical standard. The bible offered me a measuring stick to know how I was doing and where I needed to improve. Interestingly, I could never meet that standard. I could never be holy enough, so I was constantly striving to improve. There was always some area or some way that I was lacking. What I learned as I released the Christian worldview was that what I was identifying as *sin* was my human experience: anger, sadness, and lust. However, these emotions are part of what it means to be alive. The quest for holiness, as I understood it, was to set aside these human feelings and the human experience. If that standard was not met, then the person was called a *sinner* and condemned. When I let that quest for holiness go and embraced my human experience, the very behaviors I had fought as a Christian began to melt away. As I stopped seeking to meet the standard of holiness so required to be a *good* Christian, I became a better person. The bible stopped being the final word, and I let my conscience lead me. This was a scary time for me because I was not sure how I would handle the freedom of not trying to be a good Christian. My building my own moral code and making decisions based on what I feel is right has resulted in my living a life with more integrity, compassion, and self-valuation than I ever did as a Christian, and yet free of the guilt I always felt at falling short. The process of building a moral code without the aid of religion was challenging for me; I had to examine every aspect of my life and question whether the value I was proclaiming was one I believed in for myself or one I unquestioningly adopted.

One of the comforts provided by Christian religion was the possibility of life after death and the idea that anything I do not get right in this life, I can correct in heaven. The pain associated with the thought of losing my son was lessened by the idea that I would see him again in heaven. My surrendering the notion that I had eternity was challenging for me, and it was something with which I wrestled for a long time. When I accepted the mystery and the fact that there is just no way to know what comes after this life, if there is anything, I felt a rush of panic; my stomach tightened and my throat closed up as I accepted the realization that if there is no guaranteed afterlife, that means I only have the present moment. If there is no heaven, I do not have all of eternity to get it right. If there is no reincarnation, I will not be able to fulfill whatever soul contract I fail to complete in this life. I only have now.

Pondering that thought, I asked myself: If I were condemned to live the same life again, over and over, with all the same pain and pleasure, would I be happy with it? I realized that there are many things I would not want to relive and many ways of being that I do not want to carry forward. I chose to examine the areas with which I was not pleased so I could change them and create my life to be one I would be pleased to relive. The things I wanted change were many: losing patience with my children, closing my heart to love, failing to speak up, and settling for good enough instead of striving for great.

Dropping anchor in my soul

At the time of Gabriel's diagnosis, I felt my whole world shattered, as everything I thought was true changed. For years after, I tried to find something external upon which to rebuild my life: a job, career, friendship, romance, or organization. Often, just when I would feel solid, something else would happen that would shake my foundations. In my dreams of tidal waves, I clung to something solid: a post, a home, something that was deeply rooted and could withstand the storms. In my waking moments, I sought that same mooring but was unsuccessful. No matter how hard I tried, or where I looked, nothing was solid enough for me to feel anchored. As time passed, I felt more grounded, and my close friends and family reflected that sense of being grounded, but I still did not understand the deeper implications.

The answer came to me in the strangest place: while driving through a snowstorm in the mountains of Wyoming with my brother. We had been driving for more than 15 hours and still had quite a ways to go when the temperature dropped and black ice warnings started flashing. I have never liked driving in the mountains or in the snow; however, as long as I am in the driver's seat, I am generally okay. This time, however, I was in the passenger seat, exhausted because I had only had about six hours sleep in two days and had been in the car for far too many hours.

As the temperature continued to drop and the snow began to fall, I could feel the anxiety mounting in my body. It started with tightness in my solar plexus, a subtle clenching of my jaw, sweaty palms, and tension in my entire body

The anxiety quickly became terror. I was certain that I would die in that car that night. I chose to surf the waves of terror into my consciousness and wondered what message was being delivered to me.

As I listened to my inner knowledge, I heard "surrender." When I was a young child, I experienced a trauma that altered my life in significant ways. I vowed in that moment to never be vulnerable again, to never be out of control again, to never give away my power. I have spent most of my life since then managing everything about my life. When Gabriel was diagnosed with a heart defect, I was powerless, helpless, and out of control. I managed my anxiety by researching every possible thing I could and making informed decisions about his treatment. I mapped everything out and followed that plan; however, I was really rearranging chairs on a sinking ship. There was too much that I could not control no matter how hard I tried.

Thoughts raced through my head as we drove. I realized how being in the passenger seat was triggering my feelings of powerlessness and being out of control, and how difficult it was for me to tolerate those feelings.

After that happened, I began to realize what I had been missing in my journey. I was seeking solidity from outside sources. I wanted facts, data, a person, a belief system or something that I could rely on to keep me safe. I didn't trust that no matter what happened, I'd be ok. I didn't trust that I had within me what it took to survive the hardships life handed down. I didn't believe that I would be ok and so I tried to micromanage my life, hoping to avoid ever being surprised by anything. When that didn't work. I wanted someone, or something, to which I could tether myself but there was nothing or no one who could actually bear that weight.

I realized that the hero I had been seeking was somewhere within me. I had to figure out how to manage my own feelings of vulnerability, powerlessness and not being in control. There was no one person, no one organization, and no physical location that could provide me with the security I was seeking. I alone am responsible for that and as my dear friend Shawn reminded me, "Freedom is an inside job".

Finding Stability in an unstable world

I then began to struggle with how to build a stable life on constantly shifting sands. When the nature of life is unstable and made increasingly unstable with the presence of an unpredictable chronic illness in my son, I wondered whether security were possible.

That question sat inside of me and burrowed deep in my mind for quite a long time before the answer suddenly came to me. I had a mental image of myself walking through a fun house in which the floor panels are metal and the person standing on it has one foot on each panel. The floor shifts with one panel going forward and the other going back such that there is a brief moment of no movement between shifts. This is the nature of life; one moment, everything is fine, and the next, the floor shifts. The challenge is not the unending pursuit of ground that does not shift, as I had been seeking. The challenge is in learning how to stay balanced despite the shifts. As I reflected on this experience, an image of a dream I'd had of ocean waves crashing where I saw myself tethered to a post that stood strongly in the storm came into my mind. On this post, I was safe. I pondered this post and suddenly realized that it represented the truest aspects of myself. Although many things have changed in my life, many others have not. I am still kind, compassionate, loving, and honest, and I believe in doing the right thing, even when it is the hard thing. Even in the midst of trauma, I clung to my sense of who I am at the core; in the past I had called it "dropping anchor in my soul." When things were challenging, I did not have to ask myself, "What will I do?" but rather "Who will I be?"

Suddenly, the knowledge that had been inside of me in loose form solidified, and I was reminded of a palm tree, whose roots penetrate the earth so deeply that the palm is permitted to grow to great heights. The depth of the roots and the flexibility of the tree bark allow the tree to withstand hurricanes, monsoons, and some of the fiercest storms in the world. Palm trees bend in the wind, their roots holding them solidly in the ground, and when the storm passes, they regain their height, grow new leaves, and once again, reach for the sun.

The gift of grief

I also realized that part of the process of grief I experienced was necessary for me truly to transform the experience to one of joy. Grief had been a constant with me; I cried at moments of great joy because I was grateful to have the moments and also because I wondered how many more I would get with Gabriel. Although I feel that it was necessary to grieve, I also believe that by pushing the grief away and burying it for as long as I did that I prolonged the process. Perhaps it was because I was not yet ready to deal with it, but those tinges of grief colored the joyful experiences with a gray hue. I was causing my own suffering by the expectations I carried for what my child's life should look like. My friend Jason[8] wrote:

> There's the rub. Developmental disabilities . . . do not cause us (the person with the disability) to suffer. We are not victims of them. They cause *you* to suffer, because we do not match the expectations you have—a perfect child to follow in your footsteps and have perfect friends and a perfect job and one day give you perfect grandchildren. (n.p.)

Jason reminded his readers how to love someone with a disability, "Find the person, the actual person who was born to you, and love them. Fiercely. Without expectations. Let them surprise you". When I read those words, I wept as I realized how much I was inviting my own suffering because I was still grieving

---

[8] Dias, J. (2015). Asperger syndrome: why my autism makes you so nervous. Retrieved from http://anewdomain.net/2015/02/15/asperger-syndrome-autism-makes-nervous/

the loss of the "perfect" child, all the while missing the extraordinarily perfect child before me. No, Gabriel is not like other kids. He has challenges, scars, and is in many ways he is different; however, he is an amazingly compassionate, kind, sensitive child. He is always noted at school for exhibiting the kind of leadership that his teachers want all kids to emulate. Gabriel shares with his sister without hesitation and does anything I ask of him when I ask (most of the time). He loves his family, his dogs, sharks, and cheeseburgers. Gabriel has cognitive challenges, which is common in kids with heart defects; however, he is still thriving in school and is staying on track with his peers, which is quite remarkable. Gabriel has physical challenges, mainly with motor skills; however, he has been in sports for the last few years and has competed in wrestling tournaments. His life is not what I imagined it would be; I never thought I would be in this role as mother and advocate. Before Gabriel's diagnosis, I had never heard of congenital heart defects and I always believed that babies are born healthy; children grow up and outlive their parents. I was aware that bad things happened to people; however, it was always removed from me. There was never a point in my life at which I imagined that I would someday be one of those people.

Responsibility and Freedom

I also recognized that even though there are many things and circumstances over which I have no control, I have the freedom to choose how I respond to them and the meaning I create about them. In the beginning with Gabriel's diagnosis, I felt victimized by life and wondered why it was happening to me. Over time, I realized that I could choose how to see the events; I could see the diagnosis as a punishment or I could find the beauty in it. I read this story once and it reminded me of our journey:

The only survivor of a shipwreck washed up on a small, uninhabited island. He prayed feverishly for God to rescue him, and every day he scanned the horizon for help, but none seemed forthcoming. Exhausted, he eventually managed to build a little hut out of driftwood to protect him from the elements and to store his few possessions. But then one day, after scavenging for food, he arrived home to find his little hut in flames, with the smoke rolling up to the sky. The worst had happened; everything was lost. He was stung with grief and anger. "God, how could you do this to me!" he cried.

Early the next day, however, he was awakened by the sound of a ship that was approaching the island. It had come to rescue him. "How did you know I was here?" asked the weary man of his rescuers. "We saw your smoke signal," they replied.

At one point, I thought that Gabriel's diagnosis could be the worst thing that happened to me. I was devastated, just like the man whose hut burned up. I didn't realize that the devastation was actually my salvation.

I learned that what I had control over in my life was actually very little; I can control my thoughts, my feelings and my choices. This is where my power ends. When I accepted this, I also had to take responsibility for my own life and the choices I'd made up to this point. As tempting as it can be to feel like a victim to the circumstances, that is a powerless way of being. I had to accept responsibility for the choices that I'd made and the things that happened in my life. It's easy to blame others; it would be easy to blame my ex husband for his behavior but I had to go back to my own role and the ways I had contributed to the demise of the relationship. Sure, he made choices that were not beneficial but I also had my own role that I played and some of the choices I made also contributed to the end of the marriage.

When I accepted 100% responsibility for my life, choices, thoughts and feelings, I found true freedom. If I responded poorly to a situation, there was no one or nothing to blame. If I didn't like an outcome, or a situation, I realize that I am the only one who can change it. There is no magic wand, there is no fairy godmother and there is no one in the world that will change my world but me.

Oddly, accepting responsibility gave me freedom. I am not at the whim of god, or fate or anything outside of me. I am the master of my fate, the commander of my own destiny and I am fully free to choose whatever path I am on. If that path doesn't work, or I don't like a particular outcome, I am free to choose something new. When I was a child, I had a series of books I loved called "choose your own adventure". In those books, when you reached the end of a page, readers were given options on which page to turn to next. Sometimes, the outcome of that choice would be a great decision and sometimes, it would be a disaster. Before turning the page, readers had no way of knowing unless one peeked ahead (which I did sometimes). However, in life, there is no peeking ahead. There is only doing the best we have with the information we have available. When we know better, we can choose better and choosing one path doesn't mean we are stuck on that path. We are free, at any time, to change our minds, change our course and chart a new way. Nothing but death is ever final and until we take our final breath, we can always take another road. We are not free of the consequences of our choices, and we must own those choices and take responsibility for the outcomes but we are always free to choose another path, another thought or another feeling. In that sense, we are only imprisoned by our own self-imposed limitations.

This journey is not what I had planned. It is not what I would have wanted and it is not what I would have chosen. However, it is here, and it is not going anywhere. I am reminded of a quote from Fran Drescher, an actress who was diagnosed with cancer. She said, "At some point you have to stop kicking, screaming and crying, and play the hand that's been dealt to you as courageously as you possibly can".

The transformation, for me and for my family, has been in surrendering to what is, accepting what cannot be changed, and living well in spite of the challenges. There is no certainty about Gabriel's life but that is true for all of humanity. All too often, people who believe that they have plenty of time left on this Earth are killed unexpectedly. In our family, we have the gift of realizing that life is temporal. It's a double edged sword, because the awareness of my son's fragile health can be painful, but the pain serves as a reminder to remain present, stay focused on what truly matters, and to live as fully as possible.

The process that had begun in 2006 with the diagnosis of my son's heart defect was complete and I felt it within me. The scaffolding that had held me previously had crashed down around me and in the years since, I'd picked through the rubble, deciding what to keep and what to cast aside. Much had changed in that time; indeed, I am not anything like the person I was before this happened. After choosing what to keep, I had to find new beliefs and ways of seeing the world that fit this new version of me. I'd laid the new foundation, and piece by piece, rebuilt my family and myself. Like the Phoenix, I'd risen from the ashes to soar again.

Resurrection

In 2015, my family took the first of our Bucket List trips. As a family unit, we have openly discussed

Gabriel's heart health and his prognosis. Although it is scary, we each live with the awareness that each day is a gift and so we maximize it. Our Bucket List started out as a New Year's Eve vision setting exercise and Gabriel stated that he would like to go cage diving with sharks. We cut out a photo and put in on our list. Eden said she wanted to meet the Cake Boss and visit Georgetown Cupcakes, so we put that on our list.

Impulsively, I began researching shark diving companies. I found one outfit, and sent them an email, sharing that my son's bucket list wish was to go cage diving with sharks. I was asking if it was possible for an 8 year old to do such a thing. To my surprise, I got an email shortly afterward and the person responding, Michael asked me if I would be willing to share why my 8-year-old had a bucket list. I shared Gabriel's story and our commitment to live our lives to the fullest. He was deeply touched by my response and promised to get back with me soon. I didn't mention it to the kids as I didn't want to get their hopes up but I was excited. Shortly after, I got an email from Michael stating that he'd been so moved by what I'd sent him that he'd reached out to his contacts in the shark diving expedition industry and that a handful of companies replied, stating that they would be thrilled to have our family join them on an expedition. We were given a few locations to choose from including San Francisco, Cozumel, and New York.

Excited, I gathered the kids and asked Gabriel to read the email. As he read, his eyes lit up and we began exploring the options of locations and we settled on going to Montauk, New York as the chances of sighting a shark and swimming with one were the greatest. The planning had begun.

The wheels now in motion, I began to plot our journey. My mother would join us on the trip and she'd always wanted to visit New York. Eden wanted to visit New Jersey and Washington, D.C. and although I'd been to each of those places, what I most wanted was to be a part of the journey. Armed with a general idea, I went about making plans.

In June of 2015, we began the first leg of our journey, flying out of Denver to New York on a late flight. When we arrived on the plane, the pilot greeted us and the children were allowed to get in the cockpit. After we'd taken our seats, the pilot announced, "There are some special guests on board" and proceeded to tell the other travelers about our journey. Tears burned my eyes as the cabin erupted in applause and cheers. We landed in New York late at night and checked into our hotel for a brief night of sleep. A few hours later, we were off to Grand Central Station where we would board the Amtrak that would take us down the East Coast to Washington, D.C. Some hours later, we arrived in D.C., tired but excited and dropped our bags at our room. We made our first big stop on the Bucket List tour; Georgetown Cupcakes where Eden's eyes lit up as she watched the same people she adored on television making the cupcakes she'd dreamed of eating. We ordered a dozen and stayed there until Eden was ready to go.

We went back to our room and rested for the night. The next few days were spent exploring D.C. and all of its magic. At the Washington Monument, there was an elementary school visiting who happened to have two extra tickets to go to the top and the teacher generously offered to take Gabriel and Eden with her. They were so excited they could hardly contain themselves.

We took the train back up to New York City, checked into our room and went off to New Jersey where we visited Carlos Bakery, the site of the TV show Cake Boss, another one of Eden's bucket list wishes. After we left there, we went to a restaurant that bragged of the largest pizza slices in New Jersey. They weren't wrong; the slices were as big as our heads!

The following day, we were back on the Amtrak and headed out to Montauk, New York, where the following day, we would head out on our shark diving expedition. To be honest, there was a part of me that was questioning my own sanity. I'd been so fearful for Gabriel's life in the first two years that I'd hardly taken him anywhere. Now, we were trekking up and down the East Coast and in less than 24 hours, I was planning to let my eight-year-old jump into the Atlantic Ocean in a cage with a shark swimming around.

We woke early and headed to the dock where we met Michael, the man who had coordinated this event and our boat captain. It was exciting and the look on Gabriel's face told me that this was the absolute right decision to make. We headed out on the boat, passing lighthouses and other boats along the way and soon we were in the open waters. The team started chumming the waters and I crossed my fingers, hoping for a shark.

Eden spotted it first and called out, "shark!" We looked, and sure enough, a nine-foot blue shark was swimming around. Michael, who would be accompanying Gabriel in the cage told him to get ready. I don't think I'd seen Gabriel move that fast in ages. He grabbed his wetsuit and started wiggled inside. His eyes were lit up like the fourth of July and his excitement was palpable. I was so excited for him that being nervous didn't even occur to me. The captain began showing Gabriel how to use the piggyback air cylinder and how to bite to hold it in his mouth. There was a couple that was out on their own expedition and they went in the cage first. Michael was readying his camera that he was taking down with him to capture photos of Gabriel's experience.

Gabriel was patient and excited, waiting for his turn. When it finally came, Michael got in first and Gabriel slowly descended the latter. The water was freezing cold and shocked him as his bare feet touched but he never hesitated. He kept going in the water, and soon, he was fully submerged. He quickly shot to the surface, a bit disoriented from the cold and the ocean's movements but he tried again. A few tries and he finally got it; he was underwater, in the cage and watching his favorite animal swimming around him. When he popped up again and took out the ventilator, I knew he was done.

He swam to the ladder, climbed out and I began to dry him off with our towels. In his eyes, I saw delight and pride. He had done something that not many people have experienced, much less a kid of 8 years of age and I could sense in him that he'd never felt quite so alive.

The boat ride back was long and we were all beat. We sat together on the bench, Eden on one side and Gabriel on the other, and I snuggled them close.

We all fell asleep and woke shortly before getting back to shore, content and happy. It was one of the best days our family had ever experienced; it was as though we were living the life we were meant to live. There was only joy, peace and satisfaction.

We had a few more days remaining on our trip and we went back into New York City, where we explored the Empire State Building, Times Square, Rockefeller Center and of course, FAO Schwartz. My mother's dream was to visit New York City and to see the sights there, so her part of the Bucket List trip was fulfilled.

As for me, my Bucket List dream for this trip was internal...it wasn't about going somewhere or seeing something. It was about giving myself permission to live my life out loud. It was about learning how to live this way all the time. It was about letting myself be happy without the tinge of grief, or fear, or guilt or loss that I'd always felt before. I finally let myself be free.

Making Peace with Death

I won't present this image as though life has been perfect since then because it hasn't been. As I've learned, life has its challenges and those challenges will never go away. There will always be unexpected things that happen, and with a child who has a CHD, it is only wise to expect the unexpected.

There was the time where Gabriel got strep throat three times in 5 weeks, which meant he spent most of those weeks at home with me. There was the time he finally had his tonsils removed, had unexpected bleeding a week later and had to be admitted to the hospital again. When we were in the E.R., he looked at me with fear in his eyes and said, "mama, am I going to die" and I responded, hugging him "eventually, yes but not today". The shocked look on the nurse's face reminded me that many parents don't talk openly about death with their kids, but I believe that the best approach, especially in our situation is to be honest about life and death.

In our culture, especially, there is not a lot of open discussion about death. Indeed, I believe we are a death aversive culture. In many cultures around the world, death is not something kept secret and children learn from an early age that death is inevitable. In those cultures, many times, bodies are kept openly in homes and children are a part of funerals, wakes and the death ceremonies. Here, death is something to be avoided; people don't often talk about dying or the inevitability of their own death. In my own family, when my Grandmother began to age and talk about her own death, family members would say things like "oh Mom, you're not going to die!" It was bizarre to me even as a young person who realized that yes, she too would die.

Many people don't think about death or talk about death and some young people's first experience with death is when they lose a grandparent or beloved pet. In this journey of our family, I have taken an opposite stance. When my grandmother was aging, I began to feel a sense of urgency. I saw that time was ticking by and I realized that my time with her was limited so I made a deliberate point to spend time with her. I would sit for hours on end, listening to her stories, her pain, her dreams and all of the things she wanted to share. I would do her chores for her, buy her groceries and cook for her. I rubbed her feet when they ached. I knew that there would come a day that I would long for those moments so I decided not to waste them while they were still here.

When she died, I grieved but it wasn't the kind of grief that was weighted with regret. I had said what I needed to say to her, and she'd said what she needed to say to me. It was a lesson for me; I knew she was aging so I was able to finish my business with her but when Gabriel was diagnosed and after suddenly losing a number of friends who were young when they died, I realized that life is not a guarantee. I realized that although we tend to assume that we will all age and grow old, and that we all have plenty of time, that is an illusion. It was a pretty lie that I simply couldn't bring myself to buy into anymore.

In our family, we talk openly about death. We discuss the fact that our pets are aging, that my parents are aging and that as the seasons change in Colorado, so does life ever change. My children are well aware that life is temporal and while it sometimes brings them their own anticipatory grief, it also helps them to focus on what matters most. Instead of bickering with each other, a gentle reminder that "life is short, is this how you want to spend it", will often extinguish petty arguments quickly. It is our collective awareness of death that helps us to value our lives and do the things that matter. It is what helps me set aside my work, even on a deadline, to play at the park and paint little toenails.

People who most fear death are those who have never really lived. What we have found is that as we face death courageously, it has released us to fully live. When death no longer scares you, you are free to live. This approach to living and dying is not some reckless death wish; it's the realization that the only given we each have is that we will all someday die. Knowing that, the question is no longer how to avoid the inevitable but how to live defiantly and brilliantly in spite of knowing it will all eventually end.

❖

Like many kids with CHD, Gabriel has cognitive challenges that have caused him some difficulties in life. Although the research isn't clear about why there is a link between CHD and neurological difficulties, there is one and in order to best support him, I signed him for Rehabilitative psychology. Rehab psychology is a specialty area that is designed to help people with disabilities to become maximize their ability to be independent, make their own choices and to maximize their wellbeing.

Gabriel has struggled with anxiety and sometimes has difficulties making friends because his speech patterns and physical movements are often awkward. When I enlisted the support of the Rehab psychologist he worked with, it was all about helping him to navigate social challenges and managing his own feelings when challenged.

In this process, in one exercise, Gabriel was asked to identify his "armor", or times when he felt he needed to protect himself and how he would do it. Working with his rehab psychologist, he identified an aspect of himself that he calls "Gabriel the Brave". He wrote:

> Some people have new hearts, and some don't. I'm the only person in the whole school who has a new heart. Once I got a sharp sword from the Vikings and I'm now called Gabriel the Brave. I can protect me and my family with my sword. I am sometimes afraid to get blood draws but I'm not a scaredy cat. I'm not even afraid of blood. I am brave because of my new heart"

Reading this, I thought "he's going to be just fine" and now, when he is afraid or feels nervous about something, I can encourage him to send out "Gabriel the Brave" and when I do, he will close his eyes, take some deep breaths and when he opens them again, he will have a new strength within. I can almost see him stiffen his spine and get mentally prepared for whatever is to come. It's remarkable to see how resilient he is and it inspires me to be brave as well.

The long way home

In 2015, I was offered a position as a faculty member at a school in the Phoenix area and I jumped at the chance. While my life goal has always been to have my own private practice with the freedom that affords, I saw this as an opportunity to pay off debt I'd acquired during school and so we took off to a new adventure. Within three weeks of arriving, I knew I didn't want to stay in this position. The hours that I was required to work meant that I would only see my children for a short time before school started and right before they went to bed. Additionally, I discovered quickly that the insurance plan offered through this job would swallow up over a third of my salary. With that cost and daycare, financially, I was in a deficit. My back was against the wall; I'd moved my family here with high hopes and yet, I knew I couldn't continue on this path. With no small amount of fear, I quit.

The next months were quite an adventure for our family. To my surprise, when I quit the position, even though I had no safety net in place, the Universe seemed to conspire in my favor. I was invited to do segments on a local television station and my practice began to grow. Clients found me in the strangest ways and a university I'd taught with for quite some time began funneling online classes my way. We lived in a small house with a pool and we loved coming home after school to swim. Our neighbors quickly became our friends and we had a gym membership at a location we loved. Overall, life was good.

In December, however, Gabriel's insurance decided they weren't going to pay for his medicine anymore. To be clear, they refused to pay for the brand medication that is what he's always taken. The generic brands are generally pretty close to the name brand but there is enough of a difference that it can alter medication levels in the blood. For almost a month, I talked to the insurance company and the pharmacist at the specialty location that filled the medications advocated on our behalf. I reached out to Gabriel's cardiologist, asking them to send a letter to the insurance repeatedly to no avail. My frustration quickly spiraled into despair.

It went to the final hour, literally. The doctor approved the medication and spoke to the insurance that reluctantly agreed. The order was called in but it was late on a Friday, so there was no way to get it filled until Monday which meant that I had to give Gabriel a substitute medication over the weekend. I was livid and mostly, powerless. Gabriel's healthcare was the most important thing I could think of and the fact that it could be stripped away at any time, or his life saving medications denied, felt so terribly wrong.

It was then that I began considering other options. I knew in Colorado that there is a special medical program fro children with life limiting illness and that if Gabriel were enrolled on that program, he would have insurance until he was 18. Since his diagnosis, I'd been battling to keep him insured and to stay financially solvent in the process and I was simply tired of fighting. Maybe it was time to go home and to take this monkey off my back, once and for all.

For spring break, we took a trip to Long Beach, California for five days. On the way there, we stopped in Joshua Tree National Monument and marveled at the scenery. Our trip took longer than I planned because I wasn't stuck to an agenda; instead, we were in the present moment. We stopped when we needed, took photos when the scenery was right and stopped to explore.

We spent our time in California adventuring. We met friends and family for dinners and quality time. We meandered through our days, taking it easy and content to be together. We spent a day at Disneyland, arriving shortly after the gates opened and we stayed until they closed. We ate junk food, rode all the rides we were able to get on and watched the fireworks at the end of the night. The kids were asleep by the time we exited the parking garage.

We went to the beach and when we were there, Gabriel suddenly burst into tears. He said, "Mom, I hate

Arizona. I want to go home. I miss my family". The thought that had been lingering for the last few months now solidified. Living well and living without regrets is not just about going on epic adventures and taking big risks. It's also about living the day to day in a way that is meaningful. Gabriel wanted to spend his childhood near his cousins and his family. He wanted to see his grandparents more often. He wanted to live his life with the people he loved most.

For me, beyond Gabriel's desires, I recognized two things, that life is short and my parents were aging. Not only that, but my nieces and nephews were growing up so quickly and I wanted to be a part of their lives. Additionally, I realized that getting Gabriel healthcare until he is 18 would eliminate a significant amount of stress that I was carrying. It was time to release at least one thing that could lighten the load. That decision made, the process began.

This would be the third big move we'd make in as many years. It was a lot to handle for anyone, and I was concerned about the children. We spoke extensively about why this was happening and I explained to them the benefits of having insurance for Gabriel without having to deal with the threat of him losing it again. We talked about being close to family and spending more time than just holidays with our loved ones. I shared that I felt more comfortable with the transplant team in Colorado because I knew them, they knew us and I trusted them implicitly.

With a moving deadline of six weeks looming, plans began in earnest. I sold what I could, gave away the rest and we packed our belongings again. In a short time, we were ready to leave and when moving day came, the U-Haul was quickly loaded and I was off. The children flew to Colorado with my mother and I drove with the pets. I anticipated the 13 hour drive would take me about 18 hours with breaks and rest stops and I made it just as the sun was rising over the Rocky Mountains.

Coming back home was mixed for me; when I left three years earlier, it was a relief to leave it behind. I didn't ever see myself coming back to Denver and I felt a little bit of a sense of failure doing so, even though I knew I was doing the right thing for many reasons. Within weeks of being in Denver, Gabriel was enrolled on the medical program, the children were enrolled in school for the next year and I was back to work teaching. As far as transitions go, this one was seamless.

Homecoming

I quickly learned that being home was different than when I left. It wasn't as though the community had changed significantly, even though there was a lot of new growth and construction. Rather, it was me who had changed. In the process of releasing the past, and healing myself, the memories that used to be ripe with pain were now just memories, not painful.

Stolorow, a psychologist and philosopher, wrote that one of the ways in which a person can process trauma was by finding a relational home. A relational home is a place of compassion and understanding where trauma can be processed safely. When I was in Colorado before, I didn't have a relational home but I found it when I was living elsewhere. I found it in California with the relationships I cultivated throughout my doctoral program, and with the ongoing relationships I have with my Island City friends. I found it in Arizona with the friends I made there. Mostly, I found it within myself; I found that as I made space for my own healing process and learned to trust myself and be kind and gentle in the process that I was creating my own relational home.

I discovered that "home" is not a geographical location but rather, an internal condition. I came home when I finally came home to myself. I came back to Denver a changed woman—free to live, free to love and free to be completely human and still divine. No longer was I judge, jury and executioner of my own experience and myself. Now, I was a compassionate witness to living and an active participant in the manifestation of my own blessings.

Self-love

This journey revealed to me something powerful and that was that I had lacked severely in self-love. I had a point to prove and a mission to accomplish and much of what I had done before Gabriel's diagnosis was about earning love. I wanted to be loved and accepted but I didn't believe that I was lovable just as I am. I felt that love was something to be earned. When I had my children, I realized how wrong that was. I didn't love them because they did anything or because they offered me anything; I loved them simply because they existed. That realization and the understanding of how wrong I had understood love launched me into a deeper pursuit of authentic loving. Learning to be tender with myself was another facet of this path that was unexpected but welcomed.

I'm still not connected with my family outside

of very few people and I am at peace with that decision. Although there is some stigma attached with being estranged from family, I know that in order to be mentally, emotionally and spiritually happy, this is the correct path. I have learned that forgiveness does not mean that one must be in relationship with others and unconditional love doesn't mean unconditional relationship. In fact, as I grew in my own path of self-love, I realized that sometimes taking leave from people who were unable to love me, as I deserve was the most self-loving thing to do.

Forgiveness doesn't mean an automatic restoration of a relationship. In religion especially, there is the idea that forgiving someone means that you open your arms to him or her again. That is not accurate and is actually quite foolish. In order to heal a damaged relationship, the party who has caused harm must first seek restoration. There must be an accounting for behaviors and an ownership for the harm that was caused. Without that, the relationship continues to be unsafe. Unconditionally loving those people is best done from a distance. I've released the guilt and obligation that bound me to my origins and have embraced the notion that family is not only those with whom we share DNA; family are the people who show up for you when you need them. Family is the people who celebrate each other, commit to serving the highest good in the other and who will support you completely, even if they don't agree with you.

The single greatest act of self-love that I have ever engaged in is eliminating toxic relationships from my life. There is no anger behind the release; I didn't do it because I was hurt or upset. Rather, I did it because I loved myself enough to only allow those with whom I share mutual love and respect a seat in my heart. I realized that my heart is a sacred space and that only those who have earned the right can enter.

It is important for parents of children like Gabriel to know how to help our children cope and it's extremely challenging to accomplish. On the one hand, they have to know how critical it is that they take care of themselves, and on the other hand, it's important not to instill them with fear. It is a tightrope to walk. As Gabriel has gotten older, I've given him increasing responsibility for his care. He is responsible for taking his medications on time and he does this by setting an alarm on his iPod. We have spent hours together while I've taught him the names of his medications, the proper dosages and the function. When we go to the doctor now, he shares his own information.

I've also made a conscious choice with Gabriel to not "force" him to do procedures. It's important that I help him understand why he needs to have various things done and to get his agreement; without his consent, I fear he will feel as though life is happening to him and that he is a passive participant. Even with flu shots, blood draws and other painful and invasive procedures, I ask his consent.

Gabriel is an active participant in his care, and I consult with him on everything from scheduling to any medication changes. I take the time to carefully explain anything that is happening, why it needs to happen and will sit with him as long as he needs to feel comfortable. By now, he is relatively comfortable with changes but there are definitely times that have taken me by surprise and have reminded me why it's important to talk to him openly.

Recently, one of Gabriel's medications was changed and I mentioned it to him but didn't think too much about it. About a week later, Gabriel was acting out a bit so I pressed him on what was happening. He finally opened up and revealed that he was afraid that his medication wasn't working anymore and that he was dying. Stunned, I pulled him onto my lap and hugged him as he cried. I explained to him that it was only because he is growing and that as he grows, his dosages will have to change to accommodate his new size. He was somewhat assuaged but still concerned so I reached out to his transplant coordinator and she confirmed what I'd told him. She offered to get him into see the psychologist who works with the transplant team but he felt fine with the answers we had offered him.

Helping a child deal with his mortality is an incredibly painful thing and seeing my own child grapple with fear of death has rent my heart time and time again. He has a unique place in the world because unlike many kids, he is aware that his life is a miracle and that he has the potential to fall ill. That awareness is often too much for adults to bear and for a child, it's even more challenging. In Gabriel's case, we don't talk about it often but there are times when it comes crashing to the surface and we have to deal with it.

One of the times where Gabriel comes belly to belly with his mortality and the price that was paid to get to this point is when we participate in the Donor Dash. The Donor Dash is a 5k race/walk held every year in the Denver area that is designed to honor and remember donor recipients and donor families. It is an event we have participated in for the last 10 years, since

Gabriel was an infant. Each year, there is an area called the Garden of Life and in this Garden of life is a photo and dedication to Kylie, Gabriel's donor.

Each year, at the end of the race, Gabriel will head over to the Garden of Life with a drink and snack in hand and will sit with Kylie's sign. He'll gaze at her photo, and eat his snack quietly. It is a very intimate moment for him and we all stand back quietly as he sits with her. Often, he will burst into tears and will say to me "I miss Kylie. She saved my life". This is always a deeply emotional moment for everyone who witnesses it. Most often, the people witnessing this will leave in tears. Many of us will sit quietly with Gabriel until he is ready to leave which may be as short as 15 minutes and has lasted as long as an hour. This is his time, and his process, and I simply sit back and let him lead while being as supportive to him as possible.

Sometimes, Gabriel can get anxious and it seems that this is a relatively common experience for many CHD children. Although I am not aware of any studies about this, I suspect that the anxiety is rooted in their awareness of their own mortality and inadequate coping skills. Especially for those children whose parents have yet to face their own anxiety about death, the awareness lurks just beneath the surface and manifests in other ways. Gabriel gets especially anxious when he has new challenges to face, medical procedures or new things to learn but he has mastered the art of mindful breathing to help him.

Mindful breathing has been a gift for our whole family. Once I began to realize the benefits of yogic breathing for myself, I brought it to our whole family. The children began utilizing children's yoga videos and learned how to breathe deeply. One technique that works really well is to inhale deeply and when exhaling, say the word "peace". This technique is one Gabriel uses when he gets blood draws or takes exams at school and is extremely effective.

Although Gabriel is the one with the CHD, it affects our whole family. Eden has been at every appointment Gabriel has had since he was born. She knows his medications, his allergies and his needs and even though she is younger, she often acts as his caregiver. When he is sick, she wants to be with him the whole time. When he's had procedures, it impacts her deeply and cries a lot. It scares her to see her brother sick or in pain and she can hardly bear to leave his side. Many times, when he's had a procedure, she will climb in the bed with him and gently cradle his hand. She is also aware of his mortality and as a consequence, is aware of the transient nature of life as well. For Eden, it shows up most with our aging dogs;

sometimes, she will burst into tears as she imagines them dying. As with all things, I approach the aging of our pets the only way I know--directly. We have discussed our desires and have constructed a family plan for how to manage our pets' end of life care. It was a hard conversation to have, with many tears, but I felt it was necessary to have. I know that when the time comes, we will be more prepared to handle it than we would be if we didn't have a plan.

In spite of the challenges our lives have, or maybe because of the challenges, my family has a non-conventional approach to life. We don't spend a whole lot of time worried about things that don't really matter. For example, I don't place a whole lot of weight or importance on report cards or grades but tend to focus on the more important aspects of living; are my children learning? Are they being responsible? Are they kind? Are they compassionate? Mostly, I am concerned with whether they are happy.

Bonnie Ware was an Australian palliative nurse that worked with patients who were dying for over 14 years. She published a book called "Top Five Regrets of the Dying", that examined the regrets people have when they reach the end of their lives. They are:

1. I wish I had the courage to live a life true to myself and not be so concerned about what others think
2. I wish I hadn't worked so hard
3. I wish I had the courage to express my feelings
4. I wish I'd stayed in touch with my friends
5. I wish I'd let myself be happier

With those regrets in mind, I have chosen to live a life that is focused on what really matters and I lead my family the same way. It may mean that sometimes, homework is skipped because a child is tired and depleted. It may mean that laundry piles up because it's more important to go for a bike ride and play a board game. It may mean that work gets set aside. It may mean having a houseful of kids for a summer or winter break. The ways it shows up doesn't matter, really. The point is that we are committed to living so that in the end, the regrets are minimal.

Sometimes, I wonder if I'm doing it right. I have agonized over my decisions and have wondered if I screwed up along the way. I think that's probably common for any parent. I have come to the conclusion that the best measure of whether it's ok is whether I've given it my all and not whether I did my best, but whether I have done what is necessary. Before Gabriel's diagnosis, I'd never have imagined I'd have the internal resources to cope with such a big thing but I surprised myself. I found that there were reservoirs of strength within me that I'd never have reached without it. I discovered that there was a resilient, defiant spirit within me that wasn't going down without a fight.

❖

One unexpected consequence of this diagnosis is that I've had to become a fierce advocate for my son. Whether it has been ensuring that medical professionals are following hospital protocols before entering his room, or enforcing a "no flu vaccine, no visiting Gabriel" rule or advocating for teacher's who don't comply with his Individualized Education Plan (IEP), I've found a mama bear I didn't know existed before.

Gabriel doesn't look like a medically challenged kid; he is strong and healthy and because he doesn't fit the visual expectations that many have about what "sick kids" might look like, people often don't understand the seriousness of his situation. One instance stands out in particular; on his Make-A-Wish trip, Gabriel was allowed to enter the character meet and greet by the exit, so he didn't have to wait in line. In one line, a parent started making comments about how they wish they could do the same and even though Gabriel was wearing his Make-A-Wish shirt, the parent continued to make disparaging comments under his breath. I swallowed my ire and didn't say anything to him but afterward, I burst into tears and said to my mother, "I'd gladly wait in line if it meant Gabriel didn't have a heart transplant". These situations have happened more than I'd like to remember—the weight of an invisible disability is heavy.

This has required me to become an advocate; I am unabashed in my support for my child. I have gone toe-to-toe many times with doctors, educators and others who don't understand the complexity of the situation. I've also learned not to waste my time when it becomes apparent that the exercise is futile. There are those who can't or simply won't understand, and to those, I simply big adieu and move along.

❖

People often ask me how I handled my life being shattered and I often reply, "what choice did I have", but I realize I did have a choice. I could have given up and there were many times I wanted to do just that. Statistics show that having a child with a chronic illness is a factor in marriages falling apart and I'm sure that the added pressure from this added stress to an already weak marriage. Sometimes, the weight is too much and marriages can't withstand the pressure. There is no judgment; I know all too intimately how challenging it is to keep a marriage alive when it's all one can do to stay afloat emotionally.

Once giving up was no longer an option, I was faced with the choice to survive or to thrive. In the beginning, it was a moment-by-moment choice. I felt like I was running underwater and barely able to keep from drowning but every time I did something I didn't think could survive, I grew a little stronger. My faith in my own ability to rise up and face the circumstances head on increased. Soon, I stopped being afraid and stopped hating my circumstances. I no longer felt victimized or self-pitying; I realized that what happened to me could happen to anyone and that it wasn't a punishment. Over time, I realized that not only was it not a curse, it was actually a gift. It was a gift in dirty wrapping paper, one that was delivered in a damaged box. It took some time, effort and intention to be able to see beyond the "dirt" of the situation; it required that I acquire new eyes and a new vision to see beneath the surface of what happened.

It's not like it's all rainbows and sunshine. I still carry the weight of Gabriel's diagnosis and the knowledge of what that can mean for his life. Sometimes, I'll still have breakdowns and all the anger, fear and grief will come pouring out. It's not something that will ever go away—the thing with chronic illness is that it's ongoing, and because there is no foreseeable end in sight, the feelings associated will always be there. It's just that, now, it no longer consumes my life. I hold the awareness of my feelings, my fears and my grief with gentle hands but it no longer hinders me from living. The pain doesn't permeate my world on a daily basis and I am no longer paralyzed by fear. Paradoxically, perhaps, the pain and fear have liberated me from the things that used to scare me; I am no longer afraid to take risks, say what I mean, look foolish, let myself be out of control or to embrace my imperfections.

The tenuous nature of Gabriel's illness and what it's taught me about life is that ALL life is tenuous. It's tempting to think we have time; time to get our shit together, time to do what we want, time to fix the damaged relationships we have, time to figure it out, time to correct our mistakes. That is the single biggest lie that we have bought into...that there is time and so, thinking we have time, we postpone living. We delay and deny and then one day, wake up and find that there is no time left. Maybe it is waking up and realizing that you're too old to do the things you wanted to do. Maybe it's when your child leaves to college and you realize how many times you missed being fully present with them and now realize that those moments are gone. Maybe it's a tragedy that takes your loved one from you before you had a chance to tell them what they mean to you. Maybe it's all the missed opportunities to love; to laugh, to weep and to celebrate that passed by as you focused on what "needed" to be done.

The truth is that we are all on a timeline and we all have a day when there will be an end to our story but most don't have to think about it. Most don't have daily reminders in the form of medications, or appointments, to keep us aware of the limits of our lives. It doesn't change that they are there. Although it has and is still in many ways, a painful reality that we live, it has also been one of the biggest catalysts for learning how to live a meaningful life.

I wouldn't wish this on anyone because it's been and remains one of the most deeply challenging experiences of my life. It breaks my heart on a near daily basis and still, I am grateful for it happening. The last decade has been wrought with pain and transformation and yet, it has also been some of the most meaningful and special times in my life. I learned that even when I was at my lowest, I still had something within me that could keep going and I've found many ardent supporters who have held me up when I felt I couldn't go any further.

Along the way, I realized that healing and self-transformation are not a linear process but rather, a spiral process. It is not that a person heals once and then is healed forever; no, more often than not, there will be a level of healing and then we will revisit it again at some point and heal further. Things we thought we healed before may come up, raging like a river and it gives us the opportunity to heal a little more.

There is no manual for how to cope with life falling apart. There are no 10 steps to heal after devastating life experiences. There is no quick fix that will offer easy answers or a clear path to wholeness. It is a uniquely personal path and whatever happens along the way is exactly what each person needs to make his or her own way. There will be friends that come along, and friends that leave. There will be dreams that die and new ones that are born. There will be a realignment of priorities and that may require many revisions.

In japan, there is a practice wherein broken pottery is gathered and repaired along the cracks and the resin is dusted with gold powder. This practice, Kintsugi, repairs the damaged pottery in such a way that it makes it even more beautiful and valuable. It increases the value so much that there are many who have been accused of breaking pottery intentionally just so they can repair it. They realize that there is a beauty in being broken and coming back together.

There are lines on my face that weren't there ten years ago and wear on my heart and soul that have and will forever mark me. Sometimes, I look in the mirror and I see the marks that love has made on me and I don't regret their presence. The lines on my forehead may have come from long sleepless nights, rocking a sick baby and the laugh lines on the sides of my eyes have come from countless joyful members with the people I love most and who love me the same. There is an ache in my soul that is reserved for Kylie and her donor family. There is a fierceness within that has always been here but is now cultivated and refined.

Before, I wrote that I wouldn't wish this upon anyone but I have to clarify that statement. If hard times meant you'd learn how to feel pain without giving into suffering, or that you were able to live the rest of your days with a sense of irreverent awe, it would be worth it. If you could learn how to grasp tight to the things that matter and let go of the things that don't, it would be worth it. If you could learn how to sit with your own pain, and that of another and never back down, it would be worth it. If having your heart broken a million times over means that you'd be willing to boldly and unapologetically speak your truth, it would be worth it. If you could look your own deepest fear in the face, and still get up to live another day, it would be worth it.

My wish for you is that you don't have to encounter deep pain to learn how to live but that if you have, you continue to rise above the ashes and live again. Its been said that grief is the price we pay for love and as a woman who has carried, and continues to carry the weight of grief, I can attest that it is worth it. Every ounce of pain that I've felt has been far outweighed by the joy I've found. I've learned to live as though we are all dying, (because we all are) and I've never felt so alive.

As I write this, my son is lying with his head in my lap and I can feel his shoulders moving and his breathe on my skin. I hear his little sighs and can feel him relax into me. My daughter is calling for me to take her to the pool and so I end this reflection by practicing what I am preaching. I'm signing off now and going to do what truly matters.

Live.

Made in the
USA
Lexington, KY